The Book of Delight
and Other Papers
Israel Abrahams

The Book of Delight
and Other Papers

Preface

The chapters of this volume were almost all spoken addresses. The author has not now changed their character as such, for it seemed to him that to convert them into formal essays would be to rob them of any little attraction they may possess.

One of the addresses–that on "Medieval Wayfaring"–was originally spoken in Hebrew, in Jerusalem. It was published, in part, in English in the London Jewish Chronicle, and the author is indebted to the conductors of that periodical for permission to include this, and other material, in the present collection.

Some others of the chapters have been printed before, but a considerable proportion of the volume is quite new, and even those addresses that are reprinted are now given in a fuller and much revised text.

As several of the papers were intended for popular audiences, the author is persuaded that it would ill accord with his original design to overload the book with notes and references. These have been supplied only where absolutely necessary, and a few additional notes are appended at the end of the volume.

The author realizes that the book can have little permanent value. But as these addresses seemed to give pleasure to those who heard them, he thought it possible that they might provide passing entertainment also to those who are good enough to read them.

Israel Abrahams

Cambridge, Eng., September, 1911

"The Book of Delight"

Joseph Zabara has only in recent times received the consideration justly due to him. Yet his "Book of Delight," finished about the year 1200, is more than a poetical romance. It is a golden link between folk-literature and imaginative poetry. The style is original, and the framework of the story is an altogether fresh adaptation of a famous legend. The anecdotes and epigrams introduced incidentally also partake of this twofold quality. The author has made them his own, yet they are mostly adapted rather than invented. Hence, the poem is as valuable to the folklorist as to the literary critic. For, though Zabara's compilation is similar to such well-known models as the "Book of Sindbad," the Kalilah ve-Dimnah, and others of the same class, yet its appearance in Europe is half a century earlier than the translations by which these other products of the East became part of the popular literature of the Western world. At the least, then, the "Book of Delight" is an important addition to the scanty store of the folk-lore records of the early part of the thirteenth century. The folk-lore interest of the book is, indeed, greater than was known formerly, for it is now recognized as a variant of the Solomon-Marcolf legend. On this more will be said below,

As a poet and as a writer of Hebrew, Joseph Zabara's place is equally significant. He was one of the first to write extended narratives in Hebrew rhymed prose with interspersed snatches of verse, the form invented by Arabian poets, and much esteemed as the medium for story-telling and for writing social satire. The best and best-known specimens of this form of poetry in Hebrew are Charizi's Tachkemoni, and his translation of Hariri. Zabara has less art than Charizi, and far less technical skill, yet in him all the qualities are in the bud that Charizi's poems present in the fullblown flower. The reader of Zabara feels that other poets will develop his style and surpass him; the reader of Charizi knows of a surety that in him the style has reached its climax.

Of Joseph Zabara little is known beyond what may be gleaned from a discriminating study of the "Book of Delight." That this romance is largely autobiographical in fact, as it is in form, there can be no reasonable doubt. The poet writes with so much indignant warmth of the dwellers in certain cities, of their manner of life, their morals, and their culture, that one can only infer that he is relating his personal experiences. Zabara, like the hero of his romance, travelled much during the latter portion of the twelfth century, as is known from the researches of Geiger. He was born in Barcelona, and returned there to die. In the interval, we find him an apt pupil of Joseph Kimchi, in Narbonne. Joseph Kimchi, the founder of the famous Kimchi family, carried the culture of Spain to Provence; and Joseph Zabara may have acquired from Kimchi his mastery over Hebrew, which he writes with purity and simplicity. The difficulties presented in some passages of the "Book of Delight" are entirely due to the corrupt state of the text. Joseph Kimchi, who flourished in Provence from 1150 to 1170, quotes Joseph Zabara twice, with approval, in explaining verses in Proverbs. It would thus seem that Zabara, even in his student days, was devoted to the proverb-lore on which he draws so lavishly in his maturer work.

Dr. Steinschneider, to whom belongs the credit of rediscovering Zabara in modern times, infers that the poet was a physician. There is more than probability in the case; there is certainty. The romance is built by a doctor; there is more talk of medicine in it than of any other topic of discussion. Moreover, the author, who denies that he is much of a Talmudist, accepts the compliment paid to him by his visitor, Enan, that he is "skilled and well-informed in the science of medicine." There is, too, a professional tone about many of the quips and gibes in which Zabara indulges concerning doctors. Here, for instance, is an early form of a witticism that has been attributed to many recent humorists. "A philosopher," says Zabara, "was sick unto death, and his doctor gave him up; yet the patient recovered. The convalescent was walking in the street when the doctor met him. 'You come,' said he, 'from the other world.' 'Yes,' rejoined the patient, 'I come from there, and I saw there the awful retribution that falls on doctors; for they kill their patients. Yet, do not feel alarmed. You will not suffer. I told them on my oath that you are no doctor.'"

Again, in one of the poetical interludes (found only in the Constantinople edition) occurs this very professional sneer, "A doctor and the Angel of Death both kill, but the former charges a fee." Who but a doctor would enter into a scathing denunciation of the current system of diagnosis, as Zabara does in a sarcastic passage, which Erter may have imitated unconsciously? And if further proof be needed that Zabara was a man of science, the evidence is forthcoming; for Zabara appeals several times to experiment in proof of his assertions. And to make assurance doubly sure, the author informs his readers in so many words of his extensive medical practice in his native place.

If Zabara be the author of the other, shorter poems that accompany the "Book of Delight" in the Constantinople edition, though they are not incorporated into the main work, we have a further indication that Zabara was a medical man. There is a satirical introduction against the doctors that slay a man before his time. The author, with mock timidity, explains that he withholds his name, lest the medical profession turn its attention to him with fatal results. "Never send for a doctor," says the satirist, "for one cannot expect a miracle to happen." It is important, for our understanding of another feature in Zabara's work, to observe that his invective, directed against the practitioners rather than the science of medicine, is not more curious as coming from a medical man, than are the attacks on women perpetrated by some Jewish poets (Zabara among them), who themselves amply experienced, in their own and their community's life, the tender and beautiful relations that subsist between Jewish mother and son, Jewish wife and husband.

The life of Joseph ben Meïr Zabara was not happy. He left Barcelona in search of learning and comfort. He found the former, but the latter eluded him. It is hard to say from the "Book of Delight" whether he was a woman-hater, or not. On the one hand, he says many pretty things about women. The moral of the first section of the romance is: Put your trust in women; and the moral of the second section of the poem is: A good woman is the best part of man. But, though this is so, Zabara does undoubtedly quote a large number of stories full of point and sting, stories that tell of women's wickedness and infidelity, of their weakness of intellect and fickleness of will. His philogynist tags hardly compensate for his misogynist satires. He runs with the hare, but hunts energetically with the hounds.

It is this characteristic of Zabara's method that makes it open to doubt, whether the additional stories referred to as printed with the Constantinople edition did really emanate from our author's pen. These additions are sharply misogynist; the poet does not even attempt to blunt their point. They include "The Widow's Vow" (the widow, protesting undying constancy to her first love, eagerly weds another) and "Woman's Contentions." In the latter, a wicked woman is denounced with the wildest invective. She has demoniac traits; her touch is fatal. A condemned criminal is offered his life if he will wed a wicked woman. "O King," he cried, "slay me; for rather would I die once, than suffer many deaths every day." Again, once a wicked woman pursued a heroic man. He met some devils. "What are you running from?" asked they. "From a wicked woman," he answered. The devils turned and ran away with him.

One rather longer story may be summarized thus: Satan, disguised in human shape, met a fugitive husband, who had left his wicked wife. Satan told him that he was in similar case, and proposed a compact. Satan would enter into the bodies of men, and the other, pretending to be a skilful physician, would exorcise Satan. They would share the profits. Satan begins on the king, and the queen engages the confederate to cure the king within three days, for a large fee, but in case of failure the doctor is to die. Satan refuses to come out: his real plan is to get the doctor killed in this way. The doctor obtains a respite, and collects a large body of musicians, who make a tremendous din. Satan trembles. "What is that noise?" he asks. "Your wife is coming," says the doctor. Out sprang Satan and fled to the end of the earth.

These tales and quips, it is true, are directed against "wicked" women, but if Zabara really wrote them, it would be difficult to acquit him of woman-hatred, unless the stories have been misplaced, and should appear, as part of the "Book of Delight," within the Leopard section, which rounds off a series of unfriendly tales with a moral friendly to woman. In general, Oriental satire directed against women must not be taken too seriously. As Güdemann has shown, the very Jews that wrote most bitterly of women were loud in praise of their own wives–the women whom alone they knew intimately. Woman was the standing butt for men to hurl their darts at, and one cannot help feeling that a good deal of the fun got its point from the knowledge that the charges were exaggerated or untrue. You find the Jewish satirists exhausting all their stores of drollery on the subject of rollicking drunkenness. They roar till their sides creak over the humor of the wine-bibber. They laugh at him and with him. They turn again and again to the subject, which shares the empire with women in the Jewish poets. Yet we know well enough that the writers of these Hebrew Anacreontic lyrics were sober men, who rarely indulged in overmuch strong drink. In short, the medieval Jewish satirists were gifted with much of what a little time ago was foolishly styled "the new humor." Joseph Zabara was a "new" humorist. He has the quaint subtlety of the author of the "Ingoldsby Legends," and revelled in the exaggeration of trifles that is the stock-in-trade of the modern funny man. Woman plays the part with the former that the mother-in-law played a generation ago with the latter. In Zabara, again, there is a good deal of mere rudeness, which the author seems to mistake for cutting repartee. This, I take it, is another characteristic of the so-called new humor.

The probable explanation of the marked divergence between Zabara's stories and the moral he draws from them lies, however, a little deeper. The stories themselves are probably Indian in origin; hence they are marked by the tone hostile to woman so characteristic of Indian folk-lore. On the other hand, if Zabara himself was a friendly critic of woman, his own moralizings in her favor are explained. This theory is not entirely upset by the presence even of the additional stories, for these, too, are translations, and Zabara cannot be held responsible for their contents. The selection of good anecdotes was restricted in his day within very narrow limits.

Yet Zabara's reading must have been extensive. He knew something of astronomy, philosophy, the science of physiognomy, music, mathematics, and physics, and a good deal of medicine. He was familiar with Arabian collections of proverbs and tales, for he informs his readers several times that he is drawing on Arabic sources. He knew the "Choice of Pearls," the Midrashic "Stories of King Solomon," the "Maxims of the Philosophers," the "Proverbs of the Wise"; but not "Sendabar" in its Hebrew form. His acquaintance with the language of the Bible was thorough; but he makes one or two blunders in quoting the substance of Scriptural passages. Though he disclaimed the title of a Talmudic scholar, he was not ignorant of the Rabbinic literature. Everyone quotes it: the fox, the woman, Enan, and the author. He was sufficiently at home in this literature to pun therein. He also knew the story of Tobit, but, as he introduces it as "a most marvellous tale," it is clear that this book of the Apocrypha was not widely current in his day. The story, as Zabara tells it, differs considerably from the Apocryphal version of it. The incidents are misplaced, the story of the betrothal is disconnected from that of the recovery of the money by Tobit, and the detail of the gallows occurs in no other known text of the story. In one point, Zabara's version strikingly agrees with the Hebrew and Chaldee texts of Tobit as against the Greek; Tobit's son is not accompanied by a dog on his journey to recover his father's long-lost treasure.

One of the tales told by Zabara seems to imply a phenomenon of the existence of which there is no other evidence. There seems to have been in Spain a small class of Jews that were secret converts to Christianity. They passed openly for Jews, but were in truth Christians. The motive for the concealment is unexplained, and the whole passage may be merely satirical.

It remains for me to describe the texts now extant of the "Book of Delight." In 1865 the "Book of Delight" appeared, from a fifteenth century manuscript in Paris, in the second volume of a Hebrew periodical called the Lebanon. In the following year the late Senior Sachs wrote an introduction to it and to two other publications, which were afterwards issued together under the title Yen Lebanon (Paris, 1866). The editor was aware of the existence of another text, but, strange to tell, he did not perceive the need of examining it. Had he done this, his edition would have been greatly improved. For the Bodleian Library possesses a copy of another edition of the "Book of Delight," undated, and without place of issue, but printed in Constantinople, in 1577. One or two other copies of this edition are extant elsewhere. The editor was Isaac Akrish, as we gather from a marginal note to the version of Tobit given by Joseph Zabara. This Isaac Akrish was a travelling bookseller, who printed interesting little books, and hawked them about. Dr. Steinschneider points out that the date of Isaac Akrish's edition can be approximately fixed by the type. The type is that of the Jaabez Press, established in Constantinople and Salonica in 1560. This Constantinople edition is not only longer than the Paris edition, it is, on the whole, more accurate. The verbal variations between the two editions are extremely numerous, but the greater accuracy of the Constantinople edition shows itself in many ways. The rhymes are much better preserved, though the Paris edition is occasionally superior in this respect. But many passages that are quite unintelligible in the Paris edition are clear enough in the Constantinople edition.

The gigantic visitor of Joseph, the narrator, the latter undoubtedly the author himself, is a strange being. Like the guide of Gil Bias on his adventures, he is called a demon, and he glares and emits smoke and fire. But he proves amenable to argument, and quotes the story of the washerwoman, to show how it was that he became a reformed character. This devil quotes the Rabbis, and is easily convinced that it is unwise for him to wed an ignorant bride. It would seem as though Zabara were, on the one hand, hurling a covert attack against some one who had advised him to leave Barcelona to his own hurt, while, on the other hand, he is satirizing the current beliefs of Jews and Christians in evil spirits. More than one passage is decidedly anti-Christian, and it would not be surprising to find that the framework of the romance had been adopted with polemic intention.

The character of the framework becomes more interesting when it is realized that Zabara derived it from some version of the legends of which King Solomon is the hero. The king had various adventures with a being more or less demoniac in character, who bears several names: Asmodeus, Saturn, Marcolf, or Morolf. That the model for Zabara's visitor was Solomon's interlocutor, is not open to doubt. The Solomon legend occurs in many forms, but in all Marcolf (or whatever other name he bears) is a keen contester with the king in a battle of wits. No doubt, at first Marcolf filled a serious, respectable rôle; in course of time, his character degenerated into that of a clown or buffoon. It is difficult to summarize the legend, it varies so considerably in the versions. Marcolf in the best-known forms, which are certainly older than Zabara, is "right rude and great of body, of visage greatly misshapen and foul." Sometimes he is a dwarf, sometimes a giant; he is never normal. He appears with his counterpart, a sluttish wife, before Solomon, who, recognizing him as famous for his wit and wisdom, challenges him to a trial of wisdom, promising great rewards as the prize of victory. The two exchange a series of questions and answers, which may be compared in spirit, though not in actual content, with the questions and answers to be found in Zabara. Marcolf succeeds in thoroughly tiring out the king, and though the courtiers are for driving Marcolf off with scant courtesy, the king interposes, fulfils his promise, and dismisses his adversary with gifts. Marcolf leaves the court, according to one version, with the noble remark, Ubi non est lex, ibi non est rex.

This does not exhaust the story, however. In another part of the legend, to which, again, Zabara offers parallels, Solomon, being out hunting, comes suddenly on Marcolf's hut, and, calling upon him, receives a number of riddling answers, which completely foil him, and tor the solution of which he is compelled to have recourse to the proposer. He departs, however, in good humor, desiring Marcolf to come to court the next day and bring a pail of fresh milk and curds from the cow. Marcolf fails, and the king condemns him to sit up all night in his company, threatening him with death in the morning, should he fall asleep. This, of course, Marcolf does immediately, and he snores aloud. Solomon asks, "Sleepest thou?"–And Marcolf replies, "No, I think."–"What thinkest thou?"–"That there are as many vertebrae in the hare's tail as in his backbone."–The king, assured that he has now entrapped his adversary, replies: "If thou provest not this, thou diest in the morning!" Over and over again Marcolf snores, and is awakened by Solomon, but he is always thinking. He gives various answers during the night: There are as many white feathers as black in the magpie.–There is nothing whiter than daylight, daylight is whiter than milk.–Nothing can be safely entrusted to a woman.–Nature is stronger than education.

Next day Marcolf proves all his statements. Thus, he places a pan of milk in a dark closet, and suddenly calls the king. Solomon steps into the milk, splashes himself, and nearly falls. "Son of perdition! what does this mean?" roars the monarch. "May it please Your Majesty," says Marcolf, "merely to show you that milk is not whiter than daylight." That nature is stronger than education, Marcolf proves by throwing three mice, one after the other, before a cat trained to hold a lighted candle in its paws during the king's supper; the cat drops the taper, and chases the mice. Marcolf further enters into a bitter abuse of womankind, and ends by inducing Solomon himself to join in the diatribe. When the king perceives the trick, he turns Marcolf out of court, and eventually orders him to be hanged. One favor is granted to him: he may select his own tree. Marcolf and his guards traverse the valley of Jehoshaphat, pass to Jericho over Jordan, through Arabia and the Red Sea, but "never more could Marcolf find a tree that he would choose to hang on." By this device, Marcolf escapes from Solomon's hands, returns home, and passes the rest of his days in peace.

The legend, no doubt Oriental in origin, enjoyed popularity in the Middle Ages largely because it became the frame into which could be placed collections of proverbial lore. Hence, as happened also with the legend of the Queen of Sheba and her riddles, the versions vary considerably as to the actual content of the questions and answers bandied between Solomon and Marcolf. In the German and English versions, the proverbs and wisdom are largely Teutonic; in Zabara they are Oriental, and, in particular, Arabic. Again, Marcolf in the French version of Mauclerc is much more completely the reviler of woman. Mauclerc wrote almost contemporaneously with Zabara (about 1216-1220, according to Kemble). But, on the other hand, Mauclerc has no story, and his Marcolf is a punning clown rather than a cunning sage. Marcolf, who is Solomon's brother in a German version, has no trust in a woman even when dead. So, in another version, Marcolf is at once supernaturally cunning, and extremely skeptical as to the morality and constancy of woman. But it is unnecessary to enter into the problem more closely. Suffice it to have established that in Zabara's "Book of Delight" we have a hitherto unsuspected adaptation of the Solomon-Marcolf legend. Zabara handles the legend with rare originality, and even ventures to cast himself for the title rôle in place of the wisest of kings.

In the summary of the book which follows, the rhymed prose of the original Hebrew is reproduced only in one case. This form of poetry is unsuited to the English language. What may have a strikingly pleasing effect in Oriental speech, becomes, in English, indistinguishable from doggerel. I have not translated at full length, but I have endeavored to render Zabara accurately, without introducing thoughts foreign to him.

I have not thought it necessary to give elaborate parallels to Zabara's stories, nor to compare minutely the various details of the Marcolf legend with Zabara's poem. On the whole, it may be said that the parallel is general rather than specific. I am greatly mistaken, however, if the collection of stories that follows does not prove of considerable interest to those engaged in the tracking of fables to their native lairs. Here, in Zabara, we have an earlier instance than was previously known in Europe, of an intertwined series of fables and witticisms, partly Indian, partly Greek, partly Semitic, in origin, welded together by the Hebrew poet by means of a framework. The use of the framework by a writer in Europe in the year 1200 is itself noteworthy. And when it is remembered what the framework is, it becomes obvious that the "Book of Delight" occupies a unique position in medieval literature.

The Giant GuestOnce on a night, I, Joseph, lay upon my bed; sleep was sweet upon me, my one return for all my toil. Things there are which weary the soul and rest the body, others that weary the body and rest the soul, but sleep brings calm to the body and the soul at once.... While I slept, I dreamt; and a gigantic but manlike figure appeared before me, rousing me from my slumber. "Arise, thou sleeper, rouse thyself and see the wine while it is red; come, sit thee down and eat of what I provide." It was dawn when I hastily rose, and I saw before me wine, bread, and viands; and in the man's hand was a lighted lamp, which cast a glare into every corner. I said, "What are these, my master?" "My wine, my bread, my viands; come, eat and drink with me, for I love thee as one of my mother's sons." And I thanked him, but protested: "I cannot eat or drink till I have prayed to the Orderer of all my ways; for Moses, the choice of the prophets, and the head of those called, hath ordained, 'Eat not with the blood'; therefore no son of Israel will eat until he prays for his soul, for the blood is the soul...."

Then said he, "Pray, if such be thy wish"; and I bathed my hands and face, and prayed. Then I ate of all that was before me, for my soul loved him.... Wine I would not drink, though he pressed me sore. "Wine," I said, "blindeth the eyes, robbeth the old of wisdom and the body of strength, it revealeth the secrets of friends, and raiseth dissension between brothers." The man's anger was roused. "Why blasphemest thou against wine, and bearest false witness against it? Wine bringeth joy; sorrow and sighing fly before it. It strengtheneth the body, maketh the heart generous, prolongeth pleasure, and deferreth age; faces it maketh shine, and the senses it maketh bright."

"Agreed, but let thy servant take the water first, as the ancient physicians advise; later I will take the wine, a little, without water."

When I had eaten and drunk with him, I asked for his name and his purpose. "I come," said he, "from a distant land, from pleasant and fruitful hills, my wisdom is as thine, my laws as thine, my name Enan Hanatash, the son of Arnan ha-Desh." I was amazed at the name, unlike any I had ever heard. "Come with me from this land, and I will tell thee all my secret lore; leave this spot, for they know not here thy worth and thy wisdom. I will take thee to another place, pleasant as a garden, peopled by loving men, wise above all others." But I answered: "My lord, I cannot go. Here are many wise and friendly; while I live, they bear me on the wing of their love; when I die, they will make my death sweet.... I fear thee for thy long limbs, and in thy face I see, clear-cut, the marks of unworthiness; I fear thee, and I will not be thy companion, lest there befall me what befell the leopard with the fox." And I told him the story.

In this manner, illustrative tales are introduced throughout the poem. Zabara displays rare ingenuity in fitting the illustrations into his framework. He proceeds:

The Fox and the LeopardA leopard once lived in content and plenty; ever he found easy sustenance for his wife and children. Hard by there dwelt his neighbor and friend, the fox. The fox felt in his heart that his life was safe only so long as the leopard could catch other prey, and he planned out a method for ridding himself of this dangerous friendship. Before the evil cometh, say the wise, counsel is good. "Let me move him hence," thought the fox; "I will lead him to the paths of death; for the sages say, 'If one come to slay thee, be beforehand with him, and slay him instead.'" Next day the fox went to the leopard, and told him of a spot he had seen, a spot of gardens and lilies, where fawns and does disported themselves, and everything was fair. The leopard went with him to behold this paradise, and rejoiced with exceeding joy. "Ah," thought the fox, "many a smile ends in a tear." But the leopard was charmed, and wished to move to this delightful abode; "but, first," said he, "I will go to consult my wife, my lifelong comrade, the bride of my youth." The fox was sadly disconcerted. Full well he knew the wisdom and the craft of the leopard's wife. "Nay," said he, "trust not thy wife. A woman's counsel is evil and foolish, her heart hard like marble; she is a plague in a house. Yes, ask her advice, and do the opposite.".... The leopard told his wife that he was resolved to go. "Beware of the fox," she exclaimed; "two small animals there are, the craftiest they, by far–the serpent and the fox. Hast thou not heard how the fox bound the lion and slew him with cunning?" "How did the fox dare," asked the leopard, "to come near enough to the lion to do it?"

The wife than takes up the parable, and cites the incident of

The Fox and the LionThen said the leopard's wife: The lion loved the fox, but the fox had no faith in him, and plotted his death. One day the fox went to the lion whining that a pain had seized him in the head. "I have heard," said the fox, "that physicians prescribe for a headache, that the patient shall be tied up hand and foot." The lion assented, and bound up the fox with a cord. "Ah," blithely said the fox, "my pain is gone." Then the lion loosed him. Time passed, and the lion's turn came to suffer in his head. In sore distress he went to the fox, fast as a bird to the snare, and exclaimed, "Bind me up, brother, that I, too, may be healed, as happened with thee." The fox took fresh withes, and bound the lion up. Then he went to fetch great stones, which he cast on the lion's head, and thus crushed him. "Therefore, my dear leopard," concluded his wife, "trust not the fox, for I fear him and his wiles. If the place he tells of be so fair, why does not the fox take it for himself?" "Nay," said the leopard, "thou art a silly prattler. I have often proved my friend, and there is no dross in the silver of his love."

The leopard would not hearken to his wife's advice, yet he was somewhat moved by her warning, and he told the fox of his misgiving, adding, that his wife refused to accompany him. "Ah," replied the fox, "I fear your fate will be like the silversmith's; let me tell you his story, and you will know how silly it is to listen to a wife's counsel."

The Silversmith Who Followed His Wife's CounselA silversmith of Babylon, skilful in his craft, was one day at work. "Listen to me," said his wife, "and I will make thee rich and honored. Our lord, the king, has an only daughter, and he loves her as his life. Fashion for her a silver image of herself, and I will bear it to her as a gift." The statue was soon made, and the princess rejoiced at seeing it. She gave a cloak and earrings to the artist's wife, and she showed them to her husband in triumph. "But where is the wealth and the honor?" he asked. "The statue was worth much more than thou hast brought." Next day the king saw the statue in his daughter's hand, and his anger was kindled. "Is it not ordered," he cried, "that none should make an image? Cut off his right hand." The king's command was carried out, and daily the smith wept, and exclaimed, "Take warning from me, ye husbands, and obey not the voice of your wives."

The leopard shuddered when he heard this tale; but the fox went on:

The Woodcutter and the Woman A hewer of wood in Damascus was cutting logs, and his wife sat spinning by his side. "My departed father," she said, "was a better workman than thou. He could chop with both hands: when the right hand was tired, he used the left." "Nay," said he, "no woodcutter does that, he uses his right hand, unless he be a left-handed man." "Ah, my dear," she entreated, "try and do it as my father did." The witless wight raised his left hand to hew the wood, but struck his right-hand thumb instead. Without a word he took the axe and smote her on the head, and she died. His deed was noised about; the woodcutter was seized and stoned for his crime. Therefore, continued the fox, I say unto thee, all women are deceivers and trappers of souls. And let me tell you more of these wily stratagems.

The fox reinforces his argument by relating an episode in which a contrast is drawn between

Man's Love and Woman's A king of the Arabs, wise and well-advised, was one day seated with his counsellors, who were loud in the praise of women, lauding their virtues and their wisdom. "Cut short these words," said the king. "Never since the world began has there been a good woman. They love for their own ends." "But," pleaded his sages, "O King, thou art hasty. Women there are, wise and faithful and spotless, who love their husbands and tend their children." "Then," said the king, "here is my city before you: search it through, and find one of the good women of whom you speak." They sought, and they found a woman, chaste and wise, fair as the moon and bright as the sun, the wife of a wealthy trader; and the counsellors reported about her to the king. He sent for her husband, and received him with favor. "I have something for thy ear," said the king. "I have a good and desirable daughter: she is my only child; I will not give her to a king or a prince: let me find a simple, faithful man, who will love her and hold her in esteem. Thou art such a one; thou shalt have her. But thou art married: slay thy wife to-night, and to-morrow thou shalt wed my daughter." "I am unworthy," pleaded the man, "to be the shepherd of thy flock, much less the husband of thy daughter." But the king would take no denial. "But how shall I kill my wife? For fifteen years she has eaten of my bread and drunk of my cup. She is the joy of my heart; her love and esteem grow day by day." "Slay her," said the king, "and be king hereafter." He went forth from the presence, downcast and sad, thinking over, and a little shaken by, the king's temptation. At home he saw his wife and his two babes. "Better," he cried, "is my wife than a kingdom. Cursed be all kings who tempt men to sip sorrow, calling it joy." The king waited his coming in vain; and then he sent messengers to the man's shop. When he found that the man's love had conquered his lust, he said, with a sneer, "Thou art no man: thy heart is a woman's."

In the evening the king summoned the woman secretly. She came, and the king praised her beauty and her wisdom. His heart, he said, was burning with love for her, but he could not wed another man's wife. "Slay thy husband to-night, and tomorrow be my queen." With a smile, the woman consented; and the king gave her a sword made of tin, for he knew the weak mind of woman. "Strike once," he said to her; "the sword is sharp; you need not essay a second blow." She gave her husband a choice repast, and wine to make him drunken. As he lay asleep, she grasped the sword and struck him on the head; and the tin bent, and he awoke. With some ado she quieted him, and he fell asleep again. Next morning the king summoned her, and asked whether she had obeyed his orders. "Yes," said she, "but thou didst frustrate thine own counsel." Then the king assembled his sages, and bade her tell all that she had attempted; and the husband, too, was fetched, to tell his story. "Did I not tell you to cease your praises of women?" asked the king, triumphantly.

In Dispraise of Woman The fox follows up these effective narratives with a lengthy string of well-worn quotations against women, of which the following are a few: Socrates, the wise and saintly, hated and despised them. His wife was thin and short. They asked him, "How could a man like you choose such a woman for your wrife?" "I chose," said Socrates, "of the evil the least possible amount." "Why, then, do you look on beautiful women?" "Neither," said Socrates, "from love nor from desire, but to admire the handiwork of God in their outward form. It is within that they are foul." Once he was walking by the way, and he saw a woman hanging from a fig-tree. "Would," said Socrates, "that all the fruit were like this."–A nobleman built a new house, and wrote over the door, "Let nothing evil pass this way." "Then how does his wife go in?" asked Diogenes.–"Your enemy is dead," said one to another. "I would rather hear that he had got married," was the reply.

"So much," said the fox to the leopard, "I have told thee that thou mayest know how little women are to be trusted. They deceive men in life, and betray them in death." "But," queried the leopard, "what could my wife do to harm me after I am dead?" "Listen," rejoined the fox, "and I will tell thee of a deed viler than any I have narrated hitherto."

The Widow and Her Husband's Corpse The kings of Rome, when they hanged a man, denied him burial until the tenth day. That the friends and relatives of the victim might not steal the body, an officer of high rank was set to watch the tree by night. If the body was stolen, the officer was hung up in its place. A knight of high degree once rebelled against the king, and he was hanged on a tree. The officer on guard was startled at midnight to hear a piercing shriek of anguish from a little distance; he mounted his horse, and rode towards the voice, to discover the meaning. He came to an open grave, where the common people were buried, and saw a weeping woman loud in laments for her departed spouse. He sent her home with words of comfort, accompanying her to the city gate. He then returned to his post. Next night the same scene was repeated, and as the officer spoke his gentle soothings to her, a love for him was born in her heart, and her dead husband was forgotten. And as they spoke words of love, they neared the tree, and lo! the body that the officer was set to watch was gone. "Begone," he said, "and I will fly, or my life must pay the penalty of my dalliance." "Fear not, my lord," she said, "we can raise my husband from his grave and hang him instead of the stolen corpse." "But I fear the Prince of Death. I cannot drag a man from his grave." "I alone will do it then," said the woman; "I will dig him out; it is lawful to cast a dead man from the grave, to keep a live man from being thrown in." "Alas!" cried the officer, when she had done the fearsome deed, "the corpse I watched was bald, your husband has thick hair; the change will be detected." "Nay," said the woman, "I will make him bald," and she tore his hair out, with execrations, and they hung him on the tree. But a few days passed and the pair were married.

And now the leopard interlude nears it close. Zabara narrates the dénouement in these terms:

The Leopard's Fate The leopard's bones rattled while he listened to this tale. Angrily he addressed his wife, "Come, get up and follow me, or I will slay thee." Together they went with their young ones, and the fox was their guide, and they reached the promised place, and encamped by the waters. The fox bade them farewell, his head laughing at his tail. Seven days were gone, when the rains descended, and in the deep of the night the river rose and engulfed the leopard family in their beds. "Woe is me," sighed the leopard, "that I did not listen to my wife." And he died before his time.

The Journey Begun By Joseph and Enan The author has now finished his protest against his visitor's design, to make him join him on a roving expedition. Enan glares, and asks, "Am I a fox, and thou a leopard, that I should fear thee?" Then his note changes, and his tone becomes coaxing and bland. Joseph cannot resist his fascination. Together they start, riding on their asses. Then says Enan unto Joseph, "Carry thou me, or I will carry thee." "But," continues the narrator, Joseph, "we were both riding on our asses. 'What dost thou mean? Our asses carry us both. Explain thy words.'–'It is the story of the peasant with the king's officer.'"

The Clever Girl and the King's Dream A king with many wives dreamt that he saw a monkey among them; his face fell, and his spirit was troubled. "This is none other," said he, "than a foreign king, who will invade my realm, and take my harem for his spoil." One of his officers told the king of a clever interpreter of dreams, and the king despatched him to find out the meaning of his ominous vision. He set forth on his mule, and met a countryman riding. "Carry me," said the officer, "or I will carry thee." The peasant was amazed. "But our asses carry us both," he said. "Thou tiller of the earth," said the officer, "thou art earth, and eatest earth. There is snow on the hill," continued the officer, and as the month was Tammuz, the peasant laughed. They passed a road with wheat growing on each side. "A horse blind in one eye has passed here," said the officer, "loaded with oil on one side, and with vinegar on the other." They saw a field richly covered with abounding corn, and the peasant praised it. "Yes," said the officer, "if the corn is not already eaten." They went on a little further and saw a lofty tower. "Well fortified," remarked the peasant. "Fortified without, if not ruined within," replied the officer. A funeral passed them. "As to this old man whom they are burying," said the officer, "I cannot tell whether he is alive or dead." And the peasant thought his companion mad to make such unintelligible remarks. They neared a village where the peasant lived, and he invited the officer to stay with him overnight.

The peasant, in the dead of the night, told his wife and daughters of the foolish things the officer had said, though he looked quite wise. "Nay," said the peasant's youngest daughter, a maiden of fifteen years, "the man is no fool; thou didst not comprehend the depth of his meaning. The tiller of the earth eats food grown from the earth. By the 'snow on the hill' is meant thy white beard (on thy head); thou shouldst have answered, 'Time caused it.' The horse blind in one eye he knew had passed, because he saw that the wheat was eaten on one side of the way, and not on the other; and as for its burden, he saw that the vinegar had parched the dust, while the oil had not. His saying, 'Carry me, or I will carry thee,' signifies that he who beguiles the way with stories and proverbs and riddles, carries his companion, relieving him from the tedium of the journey. The corn of the field you passed," continued the girl, "was already eaten if the owner was poor, and had sold it before it was reaped. The lofty and stately tower was in ruins within, if it was without necessary stores. About the funeral, too, his remark was true. If the old man left a son, he was still alive; if he was childless, he was, indeed, dead."

In the morning, the girl asked her father to give the officer the food she would prepare. She gave him thirty eggs, a dish full of milk, and a whole loaf. "Tell me," said she, "how many days old the month is; is the moon new, and the sun at its zenith?" Her father ate two eggs, a little of the loaf, and sipped some of the milk, and gave the rest to the officer. "Tell thy daughter," he said, "the sun is not full, neither is the moon, for the month is two days old." "Ah," laughed the peasant, as he told his daughter the answers of the officer, "ah, my girl, I told you he was a fool, for we are now in the middle of the month." "Did you eat anything of what I gave you?" asked the girl of her father. And he told her of the two eggs, the morsel of bread, and the sip of milk that he had taken. "Now I know," said the girl, "of a surety that the man is very wise." And the officer, too, felt that she was wise, and so he told her the king's dream. She went back with him to the king, for she told the officer that she could interpret the vision, but would do so only to the king in person, not through a deputy. "Search thy harem," said the girl, "and thou wilt find among thy women a man disguised in female garb." He searched, and found that her words were true. The man was slain, and the women, too, and the peasant's daughter became the king's sole queen, for he never took another wife besides her.

The Night's RestThus Joseph and the giant Enan journey on, and they stay overnight in a village inn. Then commences a series of semi-medical wrangles, which fill up a large portion of the book. Joseph demands food and wine, and Enan gives him a little of the former and none of the latter. "Be still," says Enan, "too much food is injurious to a traveller weary from the way. But you cannot be so very hungry, or you would fall to on the dry bread. But wine with its exciting qualities is bad for one heated by a long day's ride." Even their asses are starved, and Joseph remarks sarcastically, "Tomorrow it will be, indeed, a case of carry-thou-me-or-I-thee, for our asses will not be able to bear us." They sleep on the ground, without couch or cover. At dawn Enan rouses him, and when he sees that his ass is still alive, he exclaims, "Man and beast thou savest, O Lord!" The ass, by the way, is a lineal descendant of Balaam's animal.

They proceed, and the asses nod and bow as though they knew how to pray. Enan weeps as they near a town. "Here," says he, "my dear friend died, a man of wisdom and judgment. I will tell thee a little of his cleverness."

The Dishonest Singer and the Wedding Robes A man once came to him crying in distress. His only daughter was betrothed to a youth, and the bridegroom and his father came to the bride's house on the eve of the wedding, to view her ornaments and beautiful clothes. When the bride's parents rose next day, everything had vanished, jewels and trousseau together. They were in despair, for they had lavished all their possessions on their daughter. My friend [continued Enan] went back with the man to examine the scene of the robbery. The walls of the house were too high to scale. He found but one place where entry was possible, a crevice in a wall in which an orange tree grew, and its edge was covered with thorns and prickles. Next door lived a musician, Paltiel ben Agan [or Adan] by name, and my late friend, the judge, interviewed him, and made him strip. His body was covered with cuts and scratches; his guilt was discovered, and the dowry returned to the last shoe-latchet. "My son," said he, "beware of singers, for they are mostly thieves; trust no word of theirs, for they are liars; they dally with women, and long after other people's money. They fancy they are clever, but they know not their left hand from their right; they raise their hands all day and call, but know not to whom. A singer stands at his post, raised above all other men, and he thinks he is as lofty as his place. He constantly emits sounds, which mount to his brain, and dry it up; hence he is so witless."

Then Enan tells Joseph another story of his friend the judge's sagacity:

The Nobleman and the Necklace A man lived in Cordova, Jacob by name, the broker; he was a man of tried honesty. Once a jewelled necklet was entrusted to him for sale by the judge, the owner demanding five hundred pieces of gold as its price. Jacob had the chain in his hand when he met a nobleman, one of the king's intimate friends. The nobleman offered four hundred pieces for the necklet, which Jacob refused. "Come with me to my house, and I will consider the price," said the would-be purchaser. The Jew accompanied him home, and the nobleman went within. Jacob waited outside the gate till the evening, but no one came out. He passed a sleepless night with his wife and children, and next morning returned to the nobleman. "Buy the necklace," said he, "or return it." The nobleman denied all knowledge of the jewels, so Jacob went to the judge. He sent for the nobles, to address them as was his wont, and as soon as they had arrived, he said to the thief's servant, "Take your master's shoe and go to his wife. Show the shoe and say, Your lord bids me ask you for the necklace he bought yesterday, as he wishes to exhibit its beauty to his friends." The wife gave the servant the ornament, the theft was made manifest, and it was restored to its rightful owner.

And Enan goes on:

The Son and the Slave A merchant of measureless wealth had an only son, who, when he grew up, said, "Father, send me on a voyage, that I may trade and see foreign lands, and talk with men of wisdom, to learn from their words." The father purchased a ship, and sent him on a voyage, with much wealth and many friends. The father was left at home with his slave, in whom he put his trust, and who filled his son's place in position and affection. Suddenly a pain seized him in the heart, and he died without directing how his property was to be divided. The slave took possession of everything; no one in the town knew whether he was the man's slave or his son. Ten years passed, and the real son returned, with his ship laden with wealth. As they approached the harbor, the ship was wrecked. They had cast everything overboard, in a vain effort to save it; finally, the crew and the passengers were all thrown into the sea. The son reached the shore destitute, and returned to his father's house; but the slave drove him away, denying his identity. They went before the judge. "Find the loathly merchant's grave," he said to the slave, "and bring me the dead man's bones. I shall burn them for his neglect to leave a will, thus rousing strife as to his property." The slave started to obey, but the son stayed him. "Keep all," said he, "but disturb not my father's bones." "Thou art the son," said the judge; "take this other as thy lifelong slave."

Joseph and Enan pass to the city of Tobiah. At the gate they are accosted by an old and venerable man, to whom they explain that they have been on the way for seven days. He invites them to his home, treats them hospitably, and after supper tells them sweet and pleasant tales, "among his words an incident wonderful to the highest degree." This wonderful story is none other than a distorted version of the Book of Tobit. I have translated this in full, and in rhymed prose, as a specimen of the original.

The Story of Tobit

Here, in the days of the saints of old, in the concourse of elders of age untold, there lived a man upright and true, in all his doings good fortune he knew. Rich was he and great, his eyes looked ever straight: Tobiah, the son of Ahiah, a man of Dan, helped the poor, to each gave of his store; whene'er one friendless died, the shroud he supplied, bore the corpse to the grave, nor thought his money to save. The men of the place, a sin-ruled race, slandering, cried, "O King, these Jewish knaves open our graves! Our bones they burn, into charms to turn, health to earn." The king angrily spoke: "I will weighten their yoke, and their villainy repay; all the Jews who, from to-day, die in this town, to the pit take down, to the pit hurry all, without burial. Who buries a Jew, the hour shall rue; bitter his pang, on the gallows shall he hang." Soon a sojourner did die, and no friends were by; but good Tobiah the corpse did lave, and dress it for the grave. Some sinners saw the deed, to the judge the word they gave, who Tobiah's death decreed. Forth the saint they draw, to hang him as by law. But now they near the tree, lo! no man can see, a blindness falls on all, and Tobiah flies their thrall. Many friends his loss do weep, but homewards he doth creep, God's mercies to narrate, and his own surprising fate, "Praise ye the Lord, dear friends, for His mercy never ends, and to His servants good intends." Fear the king distressed, his heart beat at his breast, new decrees his fear expressed. "Whoe'er a Jew shall harm," the king cried in alarm, "touching his person or personalty, touches the apple of my eye; let no man do this wrong, or I'll hang him 'mid the throng, high though his rank, and his lineage long." And well he kept his word, he punished those who erred; but on the Jews his mercies shone, the while he rilled the throne.

Once lay the saint at rest, and glanced upon the nest of a bird within his room. Ah! cruel was his doom! Into his eye there went the sparrow's excrement. Tobiah's sight was gone! He had an only son, whom thus he now addressed: "When business ventures pressed, I passed from clime to clime. Well I recall the time, when long I dwelt in Ind, of wealth full stores to find. But perilous was the road, and entrusted I my load with one of honest fame, Peër Hazeman his name. And now list, beloved son, go out and hire thee one, thy steps forthwith to guide unto my old friend's side. I know his love's full stream, his trust he will redeem; when heareth he my plight, when seeth he thy sight, then will he do the right."

The youth found whom he sought, a man by travel taught, the ways of Ind he knew; he knew them through and through, he knew them up and down, as a townsman knows his town. He brought him to his sire, who straightway did inquire, "Knowest thou an Indian spot, a city named Tobot?"–"Full well I know the place, I spent a two years' space in various enterprise; its people all are wise, and honest men and true."–"What must I give to you," asked Tobiah of his guest," to take my son in quest?"–"Of pieces pure of gold, full fifty must be told."–"I'll pay you that with joy; start forth now with my boy." A script the son did write, which Tobiah did indite, and on his son bestow a sign his friend would know. The father kissed his son, "In peace," said he, "get gone; may God my life maintain till thou art come again." The youth and guide to Tobot hied, and reached anon Peër Hazeman. "Why askest thou my name?" Straight the answer came, "Tobiah is my sire, and he doth inquire of thy health and thy household's." Then the letter he unfolds. The contents Peër espies, every doubt flies, he regards the token with no word spoken. "'Tis the son of my friend, who greeting thus doth send. Is it well with him? Say."–"Well, well with him alway."–"Then dwell thou here a while, and hours sweet beguile with the tales which thou wilt tell of him I loved so well."–"Nay, I must forthwith part to soothe my father's heart. I am his only trust, return at once I must." Peër Hazeman agrees the lad to release; gives him all his father's loan, and gifts adds of his own, raiment and two slaves. To music's pleasant staves, the son doth homeward wend. By the shore of the sea went the lad full of glee, and the wind blew a blast, and a fish was upward cast. Then hastened the guide to ope the fish's side, took the liver and the gall, for cure of evil's thrall: liver to give demons flight, gall to restore men's sight. The youth begged his friend these specifics to lend, then went he on his way to where his sick sire lay. Then spake the youth to his father all the truth. "Send not away the guide without pay." The son sought the man, through the city he ran, but the man had disappeared. Said Tobiah, "Be not afeared, 'twas Elijah the seer, whom God sent here to stand by our side, our needs to provide." He bathed both his eyes with the gall of the prize, and his sight was restored by the grace of the Lord.

Then said he to his son, "Now God His grace has shown, dost thou not yearn to do a deed in turn? My niece forthwith wed."–"But her husbands three are dead, each gave up his life as each made her his wife; to her shame and to her sorrow, they survived not to the morrow."–"Nay, a demon is the doer of this harm to every wooer. My son, obey my wish, take the liver of the fish, and burn it in full fume, at the door of her room,'twill give the demon his doom." At his father's command, with his life in his hand, the youth sought the maid, and wedded her unafraid. For long timid hours his prayer Tobiah pours; but the incense was alight, the demon took to flight, and safe was all the night. Long and happily wed, their lives sweetly sped.

Their entertainer tells Joseph and Enan another story of piety connected with the burial of the dead:

The Paralytics Touchstone of VirtueOnce upon a time there lived a saintly man, whose abode was on the way to the graveyard. Every funeral passed his door, and he would ever rise and join in the procession, and assist those engaged in the burial. In his old age his feet were paralyzed, and he could not leave his bed; the dead passed his doors, and he sighed that he could not rise to display his wonted respect. Then prayed he to the Lord: "O Lord, who givest eyes to the blind and feet to the lame, hear me from the corner of my sorrowful bed. Grant that when a pious man is borne to his grave, I may be able to rise to my feet." An angel's voice in a vision answered him, "Lo, thy prayer is heard." And so, whenever a pious man was buried, he rose and prayed for his soul. On a day, there died one who had grown old in the world's repute, a man of excellent piety, yet the lame man could not rise as his funeral passed. Next day died a quarrelsome fellow of ill fame for his notorious sins, and when his body was carried past the lame man's door, the paralytic was able to stand. Every one was amazed, for hitherto the lame man's rising or resting had been a gauge of the departed's virtue. Two sage men resolved to get to the bottom of the mystery. They interviewed the wife of the fellow who had died second. The wife confirmed the worst account of him, but added: "He had an old father, aged one hundred years, and he honored and served him. Every day he kissed his hand, gave him drink, stripped and dressed him when, from old age, he could not turn himself on his couch; daily he brought ox and lamb bones, from which he drew the marrow, and made dainty foods of it." And the people knew that honoring his father had atoned for his transgressions. Then the two inquisitors went to the house of the pious man, before whom the paralytic had been unable to rise. His widow gave him an excellent character; he was gentle and pious; prayed three times a day, and at midnight rose and went to a special chamber to say his prayers. No one had ever seen the room but himself, as he ever kept the key in his bosom. The two inquisitors opened the door of this chamber, and found a small box hidden in the window-sill; they opened the box, and found in it a golden figure bearing a crucifix. Thus the man had been one of those who do the deeds of Zimri, and expect the reward of Phineas.

Table TalkJoseph and Enan then retire to rest, and their sleep is sweet and long. By strange and devious ways they continue their journey on the morrow, starting at dawn. Again they pass the night at the house of one of Enan's friends, Rabbi Judah, a ripe old sage and hospitable, who welcomes them cordially, feeds them bountifully, gives them spiced dishes, wine of the grape and the pomegranate, and then tells stories and proverbs "from the books of the Arabs."

A man said to a sage, "Thou braggest of thy wisdom, but it came from me." "Yes," replied the sage, "and it forgot its way back."–Who is the worst of men? He who is good in his own esteem.–Said a king to a sage, "Sweet would be a king's reign if it lasted forever." "Had such been your predecessor's lot," replied the wise man, "how would you have reached the throne?"–A man laid a complaint before the king; the latter drove the suppliant out with violence. "I entered with one complaint," sighed the man, "I leave with two."–What is style? Be brief and do not repeat yourself.–The king once visited a nobleman's house, and asked the latter's son, "Whose house is better, your father's or mine?" "My father's," said the boy, "while the king is in it."–A king put on a new robe, which did not become him. "It is not good to wear," said a courtier, "but it is good to put on." The king put the robe on him.–A bore visited a sick man. "What ails thee?" he asked. "Thy presence," said the sufferer.–A man of high lineage abused a wise man of lowly birth. "My lineage is a blot on me," retorted a sage, "thou art a blot on thy lineage."–To another who reviled him for his lack of noble ancestry, he retorted, "Thy noble line ends with thee, with me mine begins."–Diogenes and Dives were attacked by robbers. "Woe is me," said Dives, "if they recognize me." "Woe is me," said Diogenes, "if they do not recognize me."–A philosopher sat by the target at which the archers were shooting. "'Tis the safest spot," said he.–An Arab's brother died. "Why did he die?" one asked. "Because he lived," was the answer.–"What hast thou laid up for the cold weather?" they asked a poor fellow. "Shivering," he answered.–Death is the dread of the rich and the hope of the poor.–Which is the best of the beasts? Woman.–Hide thy virtues as thou hidest thy faults.–A dwarf brought a complaint to his king. "No one," said the king, "would hurt such a pigmy." "But," retorted the dwarf, "my injurer is smaller than I am."–A dolt sat on a stone. "Lo, a blockhead on a block," said the passers-by.–"What prayer make you by night?" they asked a sage. "Fear God by day, and by night you will sleep, not pray."–Rather a wise enemy than a foolish friend.–Not everyone who flees escapes, not everyone who begs has need.–A sage had weak eyes. "Heal them," said they. "To see what?" he rejoined.–A fool quarrelled with a sage. Said the former, "For every word of abuse I hear from thee, I will retort ten." "Nay," replied the other, "for every ten words of abuse I hear from thee, I will not retort one."–An honest man cannot catch a thief.–All things grow with time except grief.–The character of the sent tells the character of the sender.–What is man's best means of concealment? Speech.–"Why walkest thou so slowly?" asked the lad of the greybeard. "My years are a chain to my feet: and thy years are preparing thy chain."–Do not swallow poison because you know an antidote.–The king heard a woman at prayer. "O God," she said, "remove this king from us." "And put a better in his stead," added the eavesdropping monarch.–Take measure for this life as though thou wilt live forever; prepare for the next world as though thou diest to-morrow.–"He will die," said the doctor, but the patient recovered. "You have returned from the other world," said the doctor when he met the man. "Yes," said the latter, "and the doctors have a bad time there. But fear not. Thou art no doctor."–Three things weary: a lamp that will not burn, a messenger that dawdles, a table spread and waiting.

Then follows a string of sayings about threes:

Reason rules the body, wisdom is the pilot, law is its light. Might is the lion's, burdens are the ox's, wisdom is man's; spinning the spider's, building the bee's, making stores the ant's. In three cases lying is permissible: in war, in reconciling man to man, in appeasing one's wife.

Their host concludes his lengthy list of sententious remarks thus:

A king had a signet ring, on which were engraved the words, "Thou hast bored me: rise!" and when a guest stayed too long, he showed the visitor the ring.-The heir of a wealthy man squandered his money, and a sage saw him eating bread and salted olives. "Hadst thou thought that this would be thy food, this would not be thy food."-Marry no widow. She will lament her first husband's death.

The City of Enan This was the signal for the party to retire to rest.

Next day the wayfarers reach Enan's own city, the place he had all along desired Joseph to see. He shows Joseph his house; but the latter replies, "I crave food, not sight-seeing." "Surely," says Enan, "the more hurry the less speed." At last the table is spread; the cloth is ragged, the dishes contain unleavened bread, such as there is no pleasure in eating, and there is a dish of herbs and vinegar. Then ensues a long wrangle, displaying much medical knowledge, on the physiology of herbs and vegetables, on the eating of flesh, much and fast. Enan makes sarcastic remarks on Joseph's rapacious appetite. He tells Joseph, he must not eat this or that. A joint of lamb is brought on the table, Enan says the head is bad, and the feet, and the flesh, and the fat; so that Joseph has no alternative but to eat it all. "I fear that what happened to the king, will befall thee," said Enan. "Let me feed first," said Joseph; "then you can tell me what happened to the king."

The Princess and the Rose A gardener came to his garden in the winter. It was the month of Tebet, and he found some roses in flower. He rejoiced at seeing them; and he plucked them, and put them on a precious dish, carried them to the king, and placed them before him. The king was surprised, and the flowers were goodly in his sight; and he gave the gardener one hundred pieces of gold. Then said the king in his heart, "To-day we will make merry, and have a feast." All his servants and faithful ministers were invited to rejoice over the joy of the roses. And he sent for his only daughter, then with child; and she stretched forth her hand to take a rose, and a serpent that lay in the dish leapt at her and startled her, and she died before night.

Question and Answer

But Joseph's appetite was not to be stayed by such tales as this. So Enan tells him of the "Lean Fox and the Hole"; but in vain. "Open not thy mouth to Satan," says Joseph. "I fear for my appetite, that it become smaller"; and goes on eating.

Now Enan tries another tack: he will question him, and put him through his paces. But Joseph yawns and protests that he has eaten too much to keep his eyes open.

"How canst thou sleep," said Enan, "when thou hast eaten everything, fresh and stale? As I live, thou shalt not seek thy bed until I test thy wisdom-until I prove whether all this provender has entered the stomach of a wise man or a fool."

Then follows an extraordinary string of anatomical, medical, scientific, and Talmudic questions about the optic nerves; the teeth; why a man lowers his head when thinking over things he has never known, but raises his head when thinking over what he once knew but has forgotten; the physiology of the digestive organs, the physiology of laughter; why a boy eats more than a man; why it is harder to ascend a hill than to go down; why snow is white; why babies have no teeth; why children's first set of teeth fall out; why saddest tears are saltest; why sea water is heavier than fresh; why hail descends in summer; why the sages said that bastards are mostly clever. To these questions, which Enan pours out in a stream, Joseph readily gives answers. But now Enan is hoist with his own petard.

"I looked at him," continues the poet, "and sleep entrapped his eyes, and his eyelids kissed the irides. Ah! I laughed in my heart. Now I will talk to him, and puzzle him as he has been puzzling me. He shall not sleep, as he would not let me sleep. 'My lord,' said I, 'let me now question thee.' 'I am sleepy,' said he, 'but ask on.' 'What subject shall I choose?' I said. 'Any subject,' he replied; 'of all knowledge I know the half.'" Joseph asks him astronomical, musical, logical, arithmetical questions; to all of which Enan replies, "I do not know." "But," protests Joseph, "how couldst thou assert that thou knewest half of every subject, when it is clear thou knowest nothing?" "Exactly," says Enan, "for Aristotle says, 'He who says, I do not know, has already attained the half of knowledge.'"

But he says he knows medicine; so Joseph proceeds to question him. Soon he discovers that Enan is again deceiving him; and he abuses Enan roundly for his duplicity.

Enan at length is moved to retort.

"I wonder at thy learning," says Enan, "but more at thy appetite." Then the lamp goes out, the servant falls asleep, and they are left in darkness till the morning. Then Joseph demands his breakfast, and goes out to see his ass. The ass attempts to bite Joseph, who strikes it, and the ass speaks. "I am one of the family of Balaam's ass," says the animal. "But I am not Balaam," says Joseph, "to divine that thou hast eaten nothing all night." The servant asserts that he fed the ass, but the animal had gobbled up everything, his appetite being equal to his owner's. But Joseph will not believe this, and Enan is deeply hurt. "Peace!" he shouts, and his eyes shoot flames, and his nostrils distil smoke. "Peace, cease thy folly, or, as I live, and my ancestor Asmodeus, I will seize thee with my little finger, and will show thee the city of David."

In timid tones Joseph asks him, "Who is this Asmodeus, thy kinsman?"

Enan Reveals Himself "Asmodeus," said Enan, "the great prince who, on his wing, bore Solomon from his kingdom to a distant strand." "Woe is me," I moaned, "I thought thee a friend; now thou art a fiend. Why didst thou hide thy nature? Why didst thou conceal thy descent? Why hast thou taken me from my home in guile?" "Nay," said Enan, "where was thy understanding? I gave thee my name, thou shouldst have inverted it" [i.e., transpose Desh to Shed. Enan at the beginning of the tale had announced himself as ha-Desh, he now explains that meant ha-Shed = the demon]. Then Enan gives his pedigree: "I am Enan, the Satan, son of Arnan the Demon, son of the Place of Death, son of Rage, son of Death's Shadow, son of Terror, son of Trembling, son of Destruction, son of Extinction, son of Evil-name, son of Mocking, son of Plague, son of Deceit, son of Injury, son of Asmodeus."

Nevertheless Enan quiets Joseph's fears, and promises that no harm shall befall him. He goes through Enan's city, sees wizards and sorcerers, and sinners and fools, all giants.

Enan's Friend and His Daughter

Then Enan introduces his own especial friend. "He is good and wise," said Enan, "despite his tall stature. He shows his goodness in hating the wise and loving fools; he is generous, for he will give a beggar a crust of dry bread, and make him pay for it; he knows medicine, for he can tell that if a man is buried, he either has been sick, or has had an accident; he knows astronomy, for he can tell that it is day when the sun shines, and night when the stars appear; he knows arithmetic, for he can tell that one and one make two; he knows mensuration, for he can tell how many handbreadths his belly measures; he knows music, for he can tell the difference between the barking of a dog and the braying of an ass." "But, said I," continues Joseph, "how canst thou be the friend of such a one? Accursed is he, accursed his master." "Nay," answered Enan, "I love him not; I know his vile nature: 'tis his daughter that binds me to him, for she, with her raven locks and dove's eyes and lily cheeks, is fair beyond my power to praise." Yet I warned him against marrying the daughter of an uneducated man, an Am ha-Arez. Then follows a compilation of passages directed against ignorance. "Ah!" cries Enan, "your warning moves me. My love for her is fled. Thou fearest God and lovest me, my friend. What is a friend? One heart in two bodies. Then find me another wife, one who is beautiful and good. Worse than a plague is a bad woman. Listen to what once befell me with such a one."

Thereupon Enan introduces the last of the stories incorporated into the book:

The Washerwoman Who Did the Devil's Work

Once upon a time, in my wanderings to and fro upon the earth, I came to a city whose inhabitants dwelt together, happy, prosperous, and secure. I made myself well acquainted with the place and the people, but, despite all my efforts, I was unable to entrap a single one. "This is no place for me," I said, "I had better return to my own country." I left the city, and, journeying on, came across a river, at the brink of which I seated myself. Scarcely had I done so, when a woman appeared bearing her garments to be washed in the river. She looked at me, and asked, "Art thou of the children of men or of demons?" "Well," said I, "I have grown up among men, but I was born among demons." "But what art thou after here?" "Ah," I replied, "I have spent a whole month in yonder city. And what have I found? A city full of friends, enjoying every happiness in common. In vain have I tried to put a little of wickedness among them." Then the woman, with a supercilious air: "If I am to take thee for a specimen, I must have a very poor opinion of the whole tribe of demons. You seem mighty enough, but you haven't the strength of women. Stop here and keep an eye on the wash; but mind, play me no tricks. I will go back to the city and kindle therein fire and fury, and pour over it a spirit of mischief, and thou shalt see how I can manage things." "Agreed!" said I, "I will stay here and await thy coming, and watch how affairs turn out in thy hands."

The washerwoman departed, went into the city, called upon one of the great families there residing, and requested to see the lady of the house. She asked for a washing order, which she promised to execute to the most perfect satisfaction. While the housemaid was collecting the linen, the washerwoman lifted her eyes to the beautiful face of the mistress, and exclaimed: "Yes, they are a dreadful lot, the men; they are all alike, a malediction on them! The best of them is not to be trusted. They love all women but their own wives." "What dost thou mean?" asked the lady. "Merely this," she answered. "Coming hither from my house, whom should I meet but thy husband making love to another woman, and such a hideous creature, too! How he could forsake beauty so rare and exquisite as thine for such disgusting ugliness, passes my understanding. But do not weep, dear lady, don't distress thyself and give way. I know a means by which I shall bring that husband of thine to his senses, so that thou shalt suffer no reproach, and he shall never love any other woman than thee. This is what thou must do. When thy husband comes home, speak softly and sweetly to him; let him suspect nothing; and when he has fallen asleep, take a sharp razor and cut off three hairs from his beard; black or white hairs, it matters not. These thou must afterwards give to me, and with them I will compound such a remedy that his eyes shall be darkened in their sockets, so that he will look no more upon other lovely women, but cling to thee alone in mighty and manifest and enduring love." All this the lady promised, and gifts besides for the washerwoman, should her plan prosper.

Carrying the garments with her, the woman now sought out the lady's husband. With every sign of distress in her voice and manner, she told him that she had a frightful secret to divulge to him. She knew not if she would have the strength to do so. She would rather die first The husband was all the more eager to know, and would not be refused. "Well, then," she said, "I have just been to thy house, where my lady, thy wife, gave me these garments to wash; and, while I was yet standing there, a youth, of handsome mien and nobly attired, arrived, and the two withdrew into an adjoining room: so I inclined mine ear to listen to their speech, and this is what I overheard: The young man said to thy wife, 'Kill thy husband, and I will marry thee,' She, however, declared that she was afraid to do such a dreadful deed. 'O,' answered he, 'with a little courage it is quite easy. When thy husband is asleep, take a sharp razor and cut his throat.'" In fierce rage, but suppressing all outward indication of it, the husband returned home. Pretending to fall asleep, he watched his wife closely, saw her take a razor to sever the three hairs for the washerwoman's spell, darted up suddenly, wrested the razor from her hands, and with it slew his wife on the spot.

The news spread; the relations of the wife united to avenge her death, and kill the husband. In their turn his relatives resolved to avenge him; both houses were embroiled, and before the feud was at an end, two hundred and thirty lives were sacrificed. The city resounded with a great cry, the like of which had never been heard. "From that day," concluded Enan, "I decided to injure no man more. Yet for this very reason I fear to wed an evil woman." "Fear not," returned Joseph, "the girl I recommend is beautiful and good." And Enan married her, and loved her.

Thus Enan is metamorphosed from a public demon into something of a domestic saint. Zabara gives us an inverted Faust.

Joseph Returns Home to Barcelona"After a while," concludes Joseph, "I said to him, 'I have sojourned long enough in this city, the ways of which please me not. Ignorance prevails, and poetry is unknown; the law is despised; the young are set over the old; they slander and are impudent. Let me go home after my many years of wandering in a strange land. Fain would I seek the place where dwells the great prince, Rabbi Sheshet Benveniste, of whom Wisdom says, Thou art my teacher, and Faith, Thou art my friend.' 'What qualitie,' asked Enan, 'brought him to this lofty place of righteousness and power?' 'His simplicity and humility, his uprightness and saintliness.'"

And with this eulogy of the aged Rabbi of Barcelona, the poem somewhat inconsequently ends. It may be that the author left the work without putting in the finishing touches. This would account for the extra stories, which, as was seen above, may belong to the book, though not incorporated into it.

It will be thought, from the summary mode in which I have rendered these stories, that I take Zabara to be rather a literary curiosity than a poet. But Zabara's poetical merits are considerable. If I have refrained from attempting a literal rendering, it is mainly because the rhymed-prose genre is so characteristically Oriental that its charm is incommunicable in a Western language. Hence, to those who do not read Zabara in the original, he is more easily appreciated as a conteur than as an imaginative writer. To the Hebraist, too, something of the same remark applies. Rhymed prose is not much more consistent with the genius of Hebrew than it is with the genius of English. Arabic and Persian seem the only languages in which rhymed prose assumes a natural and melodious shape. In the new-Hebrew, rhymed prose has always been an exotic, never quite a native flower. The most skilful gardeners failed to acclimatize it thoroughly in European soil. Yet Zabara's humor, his fluent simplicity, his easy mastery over Hebrew, his invention, his occasional gleams of fancy, his gift of satire, his unfailing charm, combine to give his poem some right to the title by which he called it–"The Book of Delight."

A Visit to Hebron

Of a land where every stone has its story, it can hardly be asserted that any one place has a fuller tale to tell than another. But Hebron has a peculiar old-world charm as the home of the founder of the Hebrew race. Moreover, one's youthful imagination associates Hebron with the giants, the sons of Anak, sons, that is, of the long neck; men of Arba, with broad, square shoulders. A sight of the place itself revives this memory. Ancient Hebron stood higher than the present city, but as things now are, though the hills of Judea reach their greatest elevation in the neighborhood, Hebron itself rests in a valley. Most towns in Palestine are built on hills, but Hebron lies low. Yet the surrounding hills are thirty-two hundred feet above the level of the Mediterranean, and five hundred feet higher than Mount Olivet. For this reason Hebron is ideally placed for conveying an impression of the mountainous character of Judea. In Jerusalem you are twenty-six hundred feet above the sea, but, being high up, you scarcely realize that you are in a mountain city. The hills about Hebron tower loftily above you, and seem a fitting abode for the giants whom Joshua and Caleb overthrew.

Hebron, from yet another point of view, recalls its old-world associations. Not only is Hebron one of the oldest cities in the world still inhabited, but it has been far less changed by Western influences than other famous places. Hebron is almost entirely unaffected by Christian influence. In the East, Christian influence more or less means European influence, but Hebron is still completely Oriental. It is a pity that modern travellers no longer follow the ancient route which passed from Egypt along the coast to Gaza, and then struck eastwards to Hebron. By this route, the traveller would come upon Judea in its least modernized aspect. He would find in Hebron a city without a hotel, and unblessed by an office of the Monarch of the East, Mr. Cook. There are no modern schools in Hebron; the only institution of the kind, the Mildmay Mission School, had scarcely any pupils at the time of my visit. This is but another indication of the slight effect that European forces are producing; the most useful, so far, has been the medical mission of the United Free

Church of Scotland. But Hebron has been little receptive of the educational and sanitary boons that are the chief good–and it is a great good–derived from the European missions in the East. I am almost reluctant to tell the truth, as I must, of Hebron, and point out the pitiful plight of our brethren there, lest, perchance, some philanthropists set about mending the evil, to the loss of the primitiveness in which Hebron at present revels. This is the pity of it. When you employ a modern broom to sweep away the dirt of an ancient city, your are apt to remove something else as well as the dirt.

Besides its low situation and its primitiveness, Hebron has a third peculiarity. Go where one may in Judea, the ancient places, even when still inhabited, wear a ruined look. Zion itself is scarcely an exception. Despite its fifty thousand inhabitants, Jerusalem has a decayed appearance, for the newest buildings often look like ruins. The cause of this is that many structures are planned on a bigger scale than can be executed, and thus are left permanently unfinished, or like the windmill of Sir Moses are disused from their very birth. Hebron, in this respect again, is unlike the other cities of Judea. It had few big buildings, hence it has few big ruins. There are some houses of two stories in which the upper part has never been completed, but the houses are mostly of one story, with partially flat and partially domed roofs. The domes are the result both of necessity and design; of necessity, because of the scarcity of large beams for rafters; of design, because the dome enables the rain to collect in a groove, or channel, whence it sinks into a reservoir.

Hebron, then, produces a favorable impression on the whole. It is green and living, its hills are clad with vines, with plantations of olives, pomegranates, figs, quinces, and apricots. Nowhere in Judea, except in the Jordan valley, is there such an abundance of water. In the neighborhood of Hebron, there are twenty-five springs, ten large perennial wells, and several splendid pools. Still, as when the huge cluster was borne on two men's shoulders from Eshkol, the best vines of Palestine grow in and around Hebron. The only large structure in the city, the mosque which surmounts the Cave of Machpelah, is in excellent repair, especially since 1894-5, when the Jewish lads from the Alliance school of Jerusalem renewed the iron gates within, and supplied fresh rails to the so-called sarcophagi of the Patriarchs. The ancient masonry built round the cave by King Herod, the stones of which exactly resemble the masonry of the Wailing Place in Jerusalem, still stands in its massive strength.

I have said that Hebron ought to be approached from the South or West. The modern traveller, however, reaches it from the North. You leave Jerusalem by the Jaffa gate, called by the Mohammedans Bab el-Khalil, i.e. Hebron gate. The Mohammedans call Hebron el-Khalil, City of the Friend of God, a title applied to Abraham both in Jewish and Mohammedan tradition. Some, indeed, derive the name Hebron from Chaber, comrade or friend; but Hebron may mean "confederation of cities," just as its other name, Kiriath-arba, may possibly mean Tetrapolis. The distance from Jerusalem to Hebron depends upon the views of the traveller. You can easily get to Hebron in four hours and a half by the new carriage road, but the distance, though less than twenty miles, took me fourteen hours, from five in the morning till seven at night. Most travellers turn aside to the left to see the Pools of Solomon, and the grave of Rachel lies on the right of the highroad itself. It is a modern building with a dome, and the most affecting thing is the rough-hewn block of stone worn smooth by the lips of weeping women. On the opposite side of the road is Tekoah, the birthplace of Amos; before you reach it, five miles more to the north, you get a fine glimpse also of Bethlehem, the White City, cleanest of Judean settlements. Travellers tell you that the rest of the road is uninteresting. I did not find it so. For the motive of my journey was just to see those "uninteresting" sites, Beth-zur, where Judas Maccabeus won such a victory that he was able to rededicate the Temple, and Beth-zacharias, through whose broad valley-roads the Syrian elephants wound their heavy way, to drive Judas back on his precarious base at the capital.

It is somewhat curious that this indifference to the Maccabean sites is not restricted to Christian tourists. For, though several Jewish travellers passed from Jerusalem to Hebron in the Middle Ages, none of them mentions the Maccabean sites, none of them spares a tear or a cheer for Judas Maccabeus. They were probably absorbed in the memory of the Patriarchs and of King David, the other and older names identified with this district. Medieval fancy, besides, was too busy with peopling Hebron with myths to waste itself on sober facts. Hebron, according to a very old notion, was the place where Adam and Eve lived after their expulsion from Eden; it was from Hebron's red earth that the first man was made. The Pirke di Rabbi Eliezer relate, that when the three angels visited Abraham, and he went to get a lamb for their meal, the animal fled into a cave. Abraham followed it, and saw Adam and Eve lying asleep, with lamps burning by their tombs, and a sweet savor, as of incense, emanating from the dead father and mother of human-kind. Abraham conceived a love for the Cave, and hence desired it for Sarah's resting-place.

I suppose that some will hold, that we are not on surer historical ground when we come to the Biblical statement that connects Abraham with Hebron. Before arguing whether Abraham lived in Hebron, and was buried in Machpelah, one ought to prove that Abraham ever lived at all, to be buried anywhere. But I shall venture to take Abraham's real existence for granted, as I am not one of those who think that a statement must be false because it is made in the Book of Genesis. That there was a very ancient shrine in Hebron, that the great Tree of Mamre was the abode of a local deity, may be conceded, but to my mind there is no more real figure in history than Abraham. Especially when one compares the modern legends with the Biblical story does the substantial truth of the narrative in Genesis manifest itself. The narrative may contain elements of folk poetry, but the hero Abraham is a genuine personality.

As I have mentioned the tree, it may be as well to add at once that Abraham's Oak is still shown at Hebron, and one can well imagine how it was thought that this magnificent terebinth dated from Bible times. A few years ago it was a fresh, vigorous giant, but now it is quite decayed. The ruin began in 1853, when a large branch was broken off by the weight of the snow. Twelve years ago the Russian Archimandrite of Jerusalem purchased the land on which the tree stands, and naturally he took much care of the relic. In fact, he took too much care, for some people think that the low wall which the Russians erected as a safeguard round the Oak, has been the cause of the rapid decay that has since set in. Year by year the branches have dropped off, the snow and the lightning have had their victims. It is said that only two or three years ago one branch towards the East was still living, but when I saw it, the trunk was bare and bark-less, full of little worm-holes, and quite without a spark of vitality. The last remaining fragment has since fallen, and now the site of the tree is only marked by the row of young cypresses which have been planted in a circle round the base of the Oak of Mamre. But who shall prophesy that, a century hence, a tree will not have acquired sufficient size and antiquity to be foisted upon uncritical pilgrims as the veritable tree under which Father Abraham dwelt!

The Jewish tradition does not quite agree with the view that identified this old tree with Mamre. According to Jewish tradition, the Tree is at the ruins of Ramet el-Khalil, the High Place of the Friend, i.e. of Abraham, about two miles nearer Jerusalem. Mr. Shaw Caldecott has propounded the theory that this site is Samuel's Ramah, and that the vast ruins of a stone-walled enclosure here represent the enclosure within which Samuel's altar stood. The Talmud has it that Abraham erected a guest-house for the entertainment of strangers near the Grove of Mamre. There were doors on every side, so that the traveller found a welcome from whichever direction he came. There our father made the name of God proclaimed at the mouth of all wayfarers. How? After they had eaten and refreshed themselves, they rose to thank him. Abraham answered, "Was the food mine? It is the bounty of the Creator of the Universe." Then they praised, glorified, and blessed Him who spake and the world was.

We are on the road now near Hebron, but, before entering, let us recall a few incidents in its history. After the Patriarchal age, Hebron was noted as the possession of Caleb. It also figures as a priestly city and as one of the cities of refuge. David passed much of his life here, and, after Saul's death, Hebron was the seat of David's rule over Judea. Abner was slain here by Joab, and was buried here–they still show Abner's tomb in the garden of a large house within the city. By the pool at Hebron were slain the murderers of Ishbosheth, and here Absalom assumed the throne. After his time we hear less of Hebron. Jerusalem overshadowed it in importance, yet we have one or two mentions. Rehoboam strengthened the town, and from a stray reference in Nehemiah, we gather that the place long continued to be called by its older name of Kiriath Arba. For a long period after the return from the Exile Hebron belonged to the Idumeans. It was the scene of warfare in the Maccabean period, and also during the rebellion against Rome. In the market-place at Hebron, Hadrian sold numbers of Jewish slaves after the fall of Bar-Cochba, in 135 C.E. In the twelfth century Hebron was in the hands of the Christian Crusaders. The fief of Hebron, or, as it was called, of Saint Abraham, extended southwards to Beer-sheba. A bishopric was founded there in 1169, but was abandoned twenty years later.

We hear of many pilgrims in the Middle Ages. The Christians used to eat some of the red earth of Hebron, the earth from which Adam was made. On Sunday the seventeenth of October, 1165, Maimonides was in Hebron, passing the city on his way from Jerusalem to Cairo. Obadiah of Bertinoro, in 1488, took Hebron on the reverse route. He went from Egypt across the desert to Gaza, and, though he travelled all day, did not reach Hebron from Gaza till the second morning. If the text is correct, David Reubeni was four days in traversing the same road, a distance of about thirty-three miles. To revert to an earlier time, Nachmanides very probably visited Hebron. Indeed, his grave is shown to the visitor. But this report is inaccurate. He wrote to his son, in 1267, from Jerusalem, "Now I intend to go to Hebron, to the sepulchre of our ancestors, to prostrate myself, and there to dig my grave." But he must have altered his mind in the last-named particular, for his tomb is most probably in Acre.

I need not go through the list of distinguished visitors to Hebron. Suffice it to say that in the fourteenth century there was a large and flourishing community of Jews in the town; they were weavers and dyers of cotton stuffs and glass-makers, and the Rabbi was often himself a shepherd in the literal sense, teaching the Torah while at work in the fields. He must have felt embarrassed sometimes between his devotion to his metaphorical and to his literal flock. When I was at Moza, I was talking over some Biblical texts with Mr. David Yellin, who was with me. The colonists endured this for a while, but at last they broke into open complaint. One of the colonists said to me: "It is true that the Mishnah forbids you to turn aside from the Torah to admire a tree, but you have come all the way from Europe to admire my trees. Leave the Torah alone for the present." I felt that he was right, and wondered how the Shepherd Rabbis of Hebron managed in similar circumstances.

In the century of which I am speaking, the Hebron community consisted entirely of Sefardim, and it was not till the sixteenth century that Ashkenazim settled there in large numbers.

I have already mentioned the visit of David Reubeni. He was in Hebron in 1523, when he entered the Cave of Machpelah on March tenth, at noon. It is of interest to note that his account of the Cave agrees fully with that of Conder. It is now quite certain that he was really there in person, and his narrative was not made up at second hand. The visit of Reubeni, as well as Sabbatai Zebi's, gave new vogue to the place. When Sabbatai was there, a little before the year 1666, the Jews were awake and up all night, so as not to lose an instant of the sacred intercourse with the Messiah. But the journey to Hebron was not popular till our own days. It was too dangerous, the Hebron natives enjoying a fine reputation for ferocity and brigandage. An anonymous Hebrew writer writes from Jerusalem in 1495, that a few days before a Jew from Hebron had been waylaid and robbed. But he adds: "I hear that on Passover some Jews are coming here from Egypt and Damascus, with the intention of also visiting Hebron. I shall go with them, if I am still alive."

In Baedeker, Hebron is still given a bad character, the Muslims of the place being called fanatical and violent. I cannot confirm this verdict. The children throw stones at you, but they take good care not to hit. As I have already pointed out, Hebron is completely non-Christian, just as Bethlehem is completely non-Mohammedan. The Crescent is very disinclined to admit the Cross into Hebron, the abode of Abraham, a name far more honored by Jews and Mohammedans than by Christians.

It is not quite just to call the Hebronites fanatical and sullen; they really only desire to hold Hebron as their own. "Hebron for the Hebronites" is their cry. The road, at all events, is quite safe. One of the surprises of Palestine is the huge traffic along the main roads. Orientals not only make a great bustle about what they do, but they really are very busy people. Along the roads you meet masses of passengers, people on foot, on mules and horses, on camels, in wheeled vehicles. You come across groups of pilgrims, with one mule to the party, carrying the party's goods, the children always barefooted and bareheaded–the latter fact making you realize how the little boy in the Bible story falling sick in the field exclaimed "My head, my head!" Besides the pilgrims, there are the bearers of goods and produce. You see donkeys carrying large stones for building, one stone over each saddle. If you are as lucky as I was, you may see a runaway camel along the Hebron road, scouring alone at break-neck speed, with laughter-producing gait.

Of Hebron itself I saw little as I entered, because I arrived towards sunset, and only had time to notice that everyone in the streets carried a lantern. In Jerusalem only the women carry lights, but in Hebron men had them as well. I wondered where I was to pass the night. Three friends had accompanied me from Jerusalem, and they told me not to worry, as we could stay at the Jewish doctor's. It seemed to me a cool piece of impudence to billet a party on a man whose name had been previously unknown to me, but the result proved that they were right. The doctor welcomed us right heartily; he said that it was a joy to entertain us. Now it was that one saw the advantages of the Oriental architecture. The chief room in an Eastern house is surrounded on three sides by a wide stone or wooden divan, which, in wealthy houses, is richly upholstered. The Hebron doctor was not rich, but there was the same divan covered with a bit of chintz. On it one made one's bed, hard, it is true, but yet a bed. You always take your rugs with you for covering at night, you put your portmanteau under your head as a pillow, and there you are! You may rely upon one thing. People who, on their return from Palestine, tell you that they had a comfortable trip, have seen nothing of the real life of the country. To do that you must rough it, as I did both at Modin and at Hebron. To return to the latter. The rooms have stone floors and vaulted roofs, the children walk about with wooden shoes, and the pitter-patter makes a pleasant music. They throw off the shoes as they enter the room. My host had been in Hebron for six years, and he told me overnight what I observed for myself next day, that, considering the fearful conditions under which the children live, there is comparatively little sickness. As for providing meals, a genuine communism prevails. You produce your food, your host adds his store, and you partake in common of the feast to which both sides contribute. After a good long talk, I got to sleep easily, thinking, as I dozed off, that I should pass a pleasant night. I had become impervious to the mosquitoes, but there was something else which I had forgotten. Was it a dream, an awful nightmare, or had a sudden descent of Bedouins occurred? Gradually I was awakened by a noise as of wild beasts let loose, howls of rage and calls to battle. It was only the dogs. In Jerusalem I had never heard them, as the Jewish hotel was then well out of the town; it has since been moved nearer in. It is impossible to convey a sense of the terrifying effect produced by one's first experience of the night orgies of Oriental dogs, it curdles your blood to recall it. Seen by daytime, the dogs are harmless enough, as they go about their scavenger work among the heaps of refuse and filth. But by night they are howling demons, stampeding about the streets in mad groups, barking to and at each other, whining piteously one moment, roaring hoarsely and snapping fiercely another.

The dogs did me one service, they made me get up early. I walked through a bluish-gray atmosphere. Colors in Judea are bright, yet there is always an effect as of a thin gauze veil over them. I went, then, into the streets, and at five o'clock the sun was high, and the bustle of the place had begun. The air was keen and fresh, and many were already abroad. I saw some camels start for Jerusalem, laden with straw mats made in Hebron.

Next went some asses carrying poultry for the Holy City, then a family caravan with its inevitable harem of closely veiled women. Then I saw a man with tools for hewing stone, camels coming into Hebron, a boy with a large petroleum can going to fetch water,–they are abandoning the use of the olden picturesque stone pitchers,–then I saw asses loaded with vine twigs, one with lime, women with black dresses and long white veils, boys with bent backs carrying iron stones. I saw, too, some Bethlehemite Christians hurrying home to the traditional site of the nativity. You can always distinguish these, for they are the only Christians in Palestine that wear turbans habitually. And all over the landscape dominated the beautiful green hills, fresh with the morning dew, a dew so thick that I had what I had not expected, a real morning bath. I was soaked quite wet by the time I returned from my solitary stroll. I had a capital breakfast, for which we supplied the solids, and our host the coffee. Butter is a luxury which we neither expected nor got. Hebron, none the less, seemed to me a Paradise, and I applauded the legend that locates Adam and Eve in this spot.

Alas! I had not yet seen Hebron. The doctor lived on the outskirts near the highroad, where there are many fine and beautiful residences. I was soon to enter the streets and receive a rude awakening, when I saw the manner in which the fifteen hundred Jews of Hebron live. Hebron is a ghetto in a garden; it is worse than even Jerusalem, Jerusalem being clean in comparison. Dirty, dark, narrow, vaulted, unevenly paved, running with liquid slime–such are the streets of Hebron. You are constantly in danger of slipping, unless you wear the flat, heel-less Eastern shoes, and, if you once fell, not all the perfumes of Araby could make you sweet again.

I should say that, before starting on my round, I had to secure the attendance of soldiers. Not that it was necessary, but they utilize Baedeker's assertion, that the people are savage, to get fees out of visitors–a cunning manner of turning the enemy's libels to profitable account. I hired two soldiers, but one by one others joined my train, so that by the time my tour was over, I had a whole regiment of guardians, all demanding baksheesh. I would only deal with the leader, a ragged warrior with two daggers, a sword, and a rifle. "How much?" I asked. "We usually ask a napoleon (i.e. 20 francs) for an escort, but we will charge you only ten francs." I turned to the doctor and asked him, "How much?" "Give them a beslik between them," he said. A beslik is only five pence. I offered it in trepidation, but the sum satisfied the whole gang, who thanked me profusely.

First I visited the prison, a sort of open air cage, in which about a dozen men were smoking cigarettes. The prison was much nicer than the Mohammedan school close by. This was a small overcrowded room, with no window in it, the little boys sitting on the ground, swaying with a sleepy chant. The teacher's only function was represented by his huge cane, which he plied often and skilfully. Outside the door was a barber shaving a pilgrim's head. The pilgrim was a Muslim, going on the Haj to Mecca. These pilgrims are looked on with mingled feelings; their piety is admired, but also distrusted. A local saying is, "If thy neighbor has been on the Haj, beware of him; if he has been twice, have no dealings with him; if he has been thrice, move into another street." After the pilgrim, I passed a number of blind weavers, working before large wooden frames.

But now for the Jewish quarter. This is entered by a low wooden door, at which we had to knock and then stoop to get in. The Jews are no longer forced to have this door, but they retain it voluntarily. Having got in, we were in a street so dark that we could not see a foot before us, but we kept moving, and soon came to a slightly better place, where the sun crept through in fitful gleams. The oldest synagogue was entered first. Its flooring was of marble squares, its roof vaulted, and its Ark looked north towards Jerusalem. There were, as so often in the East, two Arks; when one is too small, they do not enlarge it, but build another. The Sefardic Talmud Torah is a small room without window or ventilation, the only light and air enter by the door. The children were huddled together on an elevated wooden platform. They could read Hebrew fluently, and most of them spoke Arabic. The German children speak Yiddish; the custom of using Hebrew as a living language has not spread here so much as in Jaffa and the colonies. The Beth ha-Midrash for older children was a little better equipped; it had a stone floor, but the pupils reclined on couches round the walls. They learn very little of what we should call secular subjects. I examined the store of manuscripts, but Professor Schechter had been before me, and there was nothing left but modern Cabbalistic literature. The other synagogue is small, and very bare of ornament. The Rabbi was seated there, "learning," with great Tefillin and Tallith on–a fine, simple, benevolent soul. To my surprise he spoke English, and turned out to be none other than Rachmim Joseph Franco, who, as long ago as 1851, when the earthquake devastated the Jewish quarter, had been sent from Rhodes to collect relief funds. He was very ailing, and I could not have a long conversation with him, but he told me that he had known my father, who was then a boy, in London. Then I entered a typical Jewish dwelling of the poor. It consisted of a single room, opening on to the dark street, and had a tiny barred window at the other side. On the left was a broad bed, on the right a rude cooking stove and a big water pitcher. There was nothing else in the room, except a deep stagnant mud pool, which filled the centre of the floor.

Next door they were baking Matzoth in an oven fed by a wood fire. It was a few days before Passover. The Matzoth were coarse, and had none of the little holes with which we are familiar. So through streets within streets, dirt within dirt, room over room, in hopeless intricacy. Then we were brought to a standstill, a man was coming down the street with a bundle of wood, and we had to wait till he had gone by, the streets being too narrow for two persons to pass each other. Another street was impassable for a different reason, there was quite a river of flowing mud, knee deep. I asked for a boat, but a man standing by hoisted me on his shoulders, and carried me across, himself wading through it with the same unconcern as the boys and girls were wallowing in it, playing and amusing themselves. How alike children are all the world over!

And yet, with it all, Hebron is a healthy place. There is little of the intermittent fever prevalent in other parts of Palestine; illness is common, but not in a bad form. Jerusalem is far more unhealthy, because of the lack of water. But the Jews of Hebron are miserably poor. How they live is a mystery. They are not allowed to own land, even if they could acquire it. There was once a little business to be done in lending money to the Arabs, but as the Government refuses to help in the collection of debts, this trade is not flourishing, and a good thing, too. There are, of course, some industries. First there is the wine. I saw nothing of the vintage, as my visit was in the spring, but I tasted the product and found it good. The Arab vine-owners sell the grapes to Jews, who extract the juice. Still there is room for enterprise here, and it is regrettable that few seem to think of Hebron when planning the regeneration of Judea. True, I should regret the loss of primitiveness here, as I said at the outset, but when the lives of men are concerned, esthetics must go to the wall. The Jewish quarter was enlarged in 1875, but it is still inadequate. The Society Lemaan Zion has done a little to introduce modern education, but neither the Alliance nor the Anglo-Jewish Association has a school here. Lack of means prevents the necessary efforts from being made. Most deplorable is the fact connected with the hospital. In a beautiful sunlit road above the mosque, amid olive groves, is the Jewish hospital, ready for use, well-built, but though the very beds were there when T saw it, no patients could be received, as there were no funds. The Jewish doctor was doing a wonderful work. He had exiled himself from civilized life, as we Westerns understand it; his children had no school to which to go; he felt himself stagnating, without intellectual intercourse with his equals, yet active, kindly, uncomplaining–one of those everyday martyrs whom one meets so often among the Jews of Judea, men who day by day see their ambitions vanishing under the weight of a crushing duty. It was sad to see how he lingered over the farewell when I left him. I said that his house had seemed an oasis in the desert to me, that I could never forget the time spent with him. "And what of me?" he answered. "Your visit has been an oasis in the desert to me, but you go and the desert remains." Surely, the saddest thing in life is this feeling that one's own uninteresting, commonplace self should mean so much to others. I call it sad, because so few of us realize what we may mean to others, being so absorbed in our selfish thought of what others mean to us.

There are two industries in Hebron besides the vintage. It supplies most of the skin-bottles used in Judea, and a good deal of glassware, including lamps, is manufactured there. The Hebron tannery is a picturesque place, but no Jews are employed in it. Each bottle is made from an entire goat-skin, from which only the head and feet are removed. The lower extremities are sewn up, and the neck is drawn together to form the neck of the water bottle. Some trade is also done here in wool, which the Arabs bring in and sell at the market held every Friday. In ancient times the sheep used in the Temple sacrifices were obtained from Hebron. Besides the tannery, the glass factories are worth a visit. The one which I saw was in a cavern, lit only by the glow of the central furnace. Seated round the hearth (I am following Gautier's faithful description of the scene) and served by two or three boys, were about ten workmen, making many-colored bracelets and glass rings, which varied in size from small finger rings to circlets through which you could easily put your arm. The workmen are provided with two metal rods and a pair of small tongs, and they ply these primitive instruments with wonderful dexterity. They work very hard, at least fifteen hours a day, for five days a week.

This is one of the curiosities of the East. Either the men there are loafers, or they work with extraordinary vigor. There is nothing between doing too much and doing nothing. The same thing strikes one at Jaffa. The porters who carry your baggage from the landing stage to the steamer do more work than three English dock laborers. They carry terrific weights. When a family moves, a porter carries all the furniture on his back. Yet side by side with these overworked men, Jaffa is crowded with idlers, who do absolutely nothing. Such are the contrasts of the surprising Orient.

Many of the beads and rosaries taken to Europe by pious pilgrims are made in Hebron, just as the mother of pearl relics come chiefly from Bethlehem, where are made also the tobacco-jars of Dead Sea stone. Hebron does a fair trade with the Bedouins, but on the whole it is quite unprogressive. At first sight this may seem rather an unpleasant fact for lovers of peace. Hebron has for many centuries been absolutely free from the ravages of war, yet it stagnates. Peace is clearly not enough for progress. As the Rabbinical phrase well puts it, "Peace is the vessel which holds all other good"–without peace this other good is spilt, but peace is after all the containing vessel, not the content of happiness.

I have left out, in the preceding narrative, the visit paid to the Haram erected over the Cave of Machpelah. The mosque is an imposing structure, and rises above the houses on the hill to the left as you enter from Jerusalem. The walls of the enclosure and of the mosque are from time to time whitewashed, so that the general appearance is somewhat dazzling. It has already been mentioned that certain repairs were effected in 1894-5. The work was done by the lads of the Technical School in Jerusalem; they made an iron gate for Joseph's tomb,–the Moslems believe that Joseph is buried in Hebron,–and they made one gate for Abraham's tomb, one gate and three window gratings for Isaac's tomb, and one gate and two window gratings for Rebekah's tomb. This iron work, it is satisfactory to remember, was rendered possible by the splendid machinery sent out to the school from London by the Anglo-Jewish Association. The ordinary Jewish visitor is not allowed to enter the enclosure at all. I was stopped at the steps, where the custodian audaciously demanded a tip for not letting me in. The tombs within are not the real tombs of the Patriarchs; they are merely late erections over the spots where the Patriarchs lie buried.

No one has ever doubted that Machpelah is actually at this site, but the building is, of course, not Patriarchal in age. The enclosure is as old as the Wailing Wall at Jerusalem. It belongs to the age of Herod; we see the same cyclopean stones, with the same surface draftings as at Jerusalem. Why Herod built this edifice seems clear. Hebron was the centre of Idumean influence, and Herod was an Idumean. He had a family interest in the place, and hence sought to beautify it. No Jew or Christian can enter the enclosure except by special iradé; even Sir Moses Montefiore was refused the privilege. Rather, one should say, the Moslem authorities wished to let Sir Moses in, but they were prevented by the mob from carrying out their amiable intentions. The late English King Edward VII and the present King George V were privileged to enter the structure. Mr. Elkan Adler got in at the time when the Alliance workmen were repairing the gates, but there is nothing to see of any interest. No one within historical times has penetrated below the mosque, to the cavern itself. We still do not know whether it is called Machpelah because the Cave is double vertically or double horizontally.

The outside is much more interesting than the inside. Half way up the steps leading into the mosque, there is a small hole or window at which many Jews pray, and into which, it is said, all sorts of things, including letters to the Patriarchs, are thrown, especially by women. In the Middle Ages, they spread at this hole a tender calf, some venison pasties, and some red pottage, every day, in honor of Abraham, Isaac, and Jacob, and the food was eaten by the poor. It is commonly reported, though I failed to obtain any local confirmation of the assertion, that the Jews still write their names and their requests on strips of paper and thrust them into this hole. The Moslems let down a lamp through the hole, and also cast money into it, which is afterwards picked up by little boys as it is required for the purposes of the mosque and for repairing the numerous tombs of prophets and saints with which Hebron abounds. If you were to believe the local traditions, no corpses were left for other cemeteries. The truth is that much obscurity exists as to the identity even of modern tombs, for Hebron preserves its old custom, and none of the Jewish tombs to this day bear epitaphs. What a mass of posthumous hypocrisy would the world be spared if the Hebron custom were prevalent everywhere! But it is obvious that the method lends itself to inventiveness, and as the tombs are unnamed, local guides tell you anything they choose about them, and you do not believe them even when they are speaking the truth.

There is only one other fact to tell about the Cave. The Moslems have a curious dread of Isaac and Rebekah, they regard the other Patriarchs as kindly disposed, but Isaac is irritable, and Rebekah malicious. It is told of Ibrahim Pasha of Egypt, he who "feared neither man nor devil," that when he was let down into the Cave by a rope, he surprised Rebekah in the act of combing her hair. She resented the intrusion, and gave him so severe a box on the ears that he fell down in a fit, and could be rescued alive only with much difficulty. It is with equal difficulty that one can depart, with any reverence left, from the mass of legend and childishness with which one is crushed in such places. One escapes with the thought of the real Abraham, his glorious service to humanity, his lifelong devotion to the making of souls, to the spread of the knowledge of God. One recalls the Abraham who, in the Jewish tradition, is the type of unselfishness, of watchfulness on behalf of his descendants, the marks of whose genuine relationship to the Patriarch are a generous eye and a humble spirit. As one turns from Hebron, full of such happy memories, one forms the resolve not to rely solely on an appeal to the Patriarch's merits, but to strive to do something oneself for the Jewish cause, and thus fulfil the poet's lines,

> Thus shalt thou plant a garden round the tomb,
> Where golden hopes may flower, and fruits immortal bloom.

The Solace of Books

In the year 1190, Judah ibn Tibbon, a famous Provençal Jew, who had migrated to Southern France from Granada, wrote in Hebrew as follows to his son:

"Avoid bad society: make thy books thy companions. Let thy bookcases and shelves be thy gardens and pleasure grounds. Pluck the fruit that grows therein; gather the roses, the spices, and the myrrh. If thy soul be satiate and weary, change from garden to garden, from furrow to furrow, from scene to scene. Then shall thy desire renew itself, and thy soul be rich with manifold delight."

In this beautiful comparison of a library to a garden, there is one point missing. The perfection of enjoyment is reached when the library, or at least a portable part of it, is actually carried into the garden. When Lightfoot was residing at Ashley (Staffordshire), he followed this course, as we know from a letter of his biographer. "There he built himself a small house in the midst of a garden, containing two rooms below, viz. a study and a withdrawing room, and a lodging chamber above; and there he studied hard, and laid the foundations of his Rabbinic learning, and took great delight, lodging there often, though [quaintly adds John Stype] he was then a married man." Montaigne, whose great-grandfather, be it recalled, was a Spanish Jew, did not possess a library built in the open air, but he had the next best thing. He used the top story of a tower, whence, says he, "I behold under me my garden."

In ancient Athens, philosophers thought out their grandest ideas walking up and down their groves. Nature sobers us. "When I behold Thy heavens, the work of Thy fingers, the moon and the stars which Thou hast ordained; what is man that Thou art mindful of him, and the son of man that Thou visitest him?" But if nature sobers, she also consoles. As the Psalmist continues: "Thou hast made him but little lower than the angels, and crownest him with glory and honor. Thou madest him to have dominion over the works of Thy hands; Thou hast put all things under his feet." Face to face with nature, man realizes that he is greater than she. "On earth there is nothing great but man, in man there is nothing great but mind." So, no doubt, the Athenian sages gained courage as well as modesty from the contact of mind with nature. And not they only, for our own Jewish treasure, the Mishnah, grew up, if not literally, at least metaphorically, in the open air, in the vineyard of Jamnia. Standing in the sordid little village which to-day occupies the site of ancient Jamnia, with the sea close at hand and the plain of Sharon and the Judean lowlands at my feet, I could see Rabbi Jochanan ben Zakkai and his comrades pacing to and fro, pondering those great thoughts which live among us now, though the authors of them have been in their graves for eighteen centuries.

It is curious how often this habit of movement goes with thinking. Montaigne says: "Every place of retirement requires a Walk. My thoughts sleep if I sit still; my Fancy does not go by itself, as it goes when my Legs move it." What Montaigne seems to mean is that we love rhythm. Body and mind must move together in harmony. So it is with the Mohammedan over the Koran, and the Rabbi over the Talmud. Jews sway at prayer for the same reason. Movement of the body is not a mere mannerism; it is part of the emotion, like the instrumental accompaniment to a song. The child cons his lesson moving; we foolishly call it "fidgeting." The child is never receptive unless also active. But there is another of Montaigne's feelings, with which I have no sympathy. He loved to think when on the move, but his walk must be solitary. "'Tis here," he says of his library, "I am in my kingdom, and I endeavor to make myself an absolute monarch. So I sequester this one corner from all society–conjugal, filial, civil." This is a detestable habit. It is the acme of selfishness, to shut yourself up with your books. To write over your study door "Let no one enter here!" is to proclaim your work divorced from life. Montaigne gloried in the inaccessibility of his asylum. His house was perched upon an "overpeering hillock," so that in any part of it–still more in the round room of the tower–he could "the better seclude myself from company, and keep encroachers from me." Yet some may work best when there are others beside them. From the book the reader turns to the child that prattles near, and realizes how much more the child can ask than the book can answer. The presence of the young living soul corrects the vanity of the dead old pedant. Books are most solacing when the limitations of bookish wisdom are perceived. "Literature," said Matthew Arnold, "is a criticism of life." This is true, despite the objections of Saintsbury, but I venture to add that "life is a criticism of literature."

Now, I am not going to convert a paper on the Solace of Books into a paper in dispraise of books. I shall not be so untrue to my theme. But I give fair warning that I shall make no attempt to scale the height or sound the depth of the intellectual phases of this great subject. I invite my reader only to dally desultorily on the gentler slopes of sentiment.

One of the most comforting qualities of books has been well expressed by Richard of Bury in his famous Philobiblon, written in 1344. This is an exquisite little volume on the Love of Books, which Mr. Israel Gollancz has now edited in an exquisite edition, attainable for the sum of one shilling. "How safely," says Richard, "we lay bare the poverty of human ignorance to books, without feeling any shame."

Then he goes on to describe books as those silent teachers who "instruct us without rods or stripes; without taunts or anger; without gifts or money; who are not asleep when we approach them, and do not deny us when we question them; who do not chide us when we err, or laugh at us if we are ignorant."

It is Richard of Bury's last phrase that I find so solacing. No one is ever ashamed of turning to a book, but many hesitate to admit their ignorance to an interlocutor. Your dictionary, your encyclopedia, and your other books, are the recipients of many a silent confession of nescience which you would never dream of making auricular. You go to these "golden pots in which manna is stored," and extract food exactly to your passing taste, without needing to admit, as Esau did to Jacob, that you are hungry unto death. This comparison of books to food is of itself solacing, for there is always something attractive in metaphors drawn from the delights of the table. The metaphor is very old.

"Open thy mouth," said the Lord to Ezekiel, "and eat that which I give thee. And when I looked, a hand was put forth unto me, and, lo, a scroll of a book was therein.... Then I did eat it, and it was in my mouth as honey for sweetness."

What a quaint use does Richard of Bury make of this very passage! Addressing the clergy, he says "Eat the book with Ezekiel, that the belly of your memory may be sweetened within, and thus, as with the panther refreshed, to whose breath all beasts and cattle long to approach, the sweet savor of the spices it has eaten may shed a perfume without."

Willing enough would I be to devote the whole of my paper to Richard of Bury. I must, however, content myself with one other noble extract, which, I hope, will whet my reader's appetite for more: "Moses, the gentlest of men, teaches us to make bookcases most neatly, wherein they [books] may be protected from any injury. Take, he says, this book of the Law and put it in the side of the Ark of the Covenant of the Lord your God. O fitting place and appropriate for a library, which was made of imperishable shittim [i.e. acacia] wood, and was covered within and without with gold."

Still we must not push this idea of costly bookcases too far. Judah the Pious wrote in the twelfth century, "Books were made for use, not to be hidden away." This reminds me that Richard of Bury is not the only medieval book-lover with whom we might spend a pleasant evening. Judah ben Samuel Sir Leon, surnamed the Pious, whom I have just quoted, wrote the "Book of the Pious" in Hebrew, in 1190, and it has many excellent paragraphs about books. Judah's subject is, however, the care of books rather than the solace derivable from them. Still, he comes into my theme, for few people can have enjoyed books more than he. He had no selfish love for them: he not only possessed books, he lent them. He was a very prince of book-lenders, for he did not object if the borrowers of his books re-lent them in their turn. So, on dying, he advised his sons to lend his books even to an enemy (par. 876). "If a father dies," he says elsewhere (par. 919), "and leaves a dog and a book to his sons, one shall not say to the other, You take the dog, and I'll take the book," as though the two were comparable in value. Poor, primitive Judah the Pious! We wiser moderns should never dream of making the comparison between a dog and a book, but for the opposite reason. Judah shrank from equalling a book to a dog, but we know better than to undervalue a dog so far as to compare it with a book. The kennel costs more than the bookcase, and love of dogs is a higher solace than love of books. To those who think thus, what more convincing condemnation of books could be formulated than the phrase coined by Gilbert de Porre in praise of his library, "It is a garden of immortal fruits, without dog or dragon."

I meant to part with Richard of Bury, but I must ask permission to revert to him. Some of the delight he felt in books arose from his preference of reading to oral intercourse. "The truth in speech perishes with the sound: it is patent to the ear only and eludes the sight: begins and perishes as it were in a breath." Personally I share this view, and I believe firmly that the written word brings more pleasure than the spoken word.

Plato held the opposite view. He would have agreed with the advice given by Chesterfield to his son, "Lay aside the best book when you can go into the best company–depend upon it you change for the better." Plato did, indeed, characterize books as "immortal sons deifying their sires." But, on the opposite side, he has that memorable passage, part of which I now quote, from the same source that has supplied several others of my quotations, Mr. Alexander Ireland's "Book-Lover's Enchiridion." "Writing," says Plato, "has this terrible disadvantage, which puts it on the same footing with painting. The artist's productions stand before you, as if they were alive: but if you ask them anything, they keep a solemn silence. Just so with written discourse: you would fancy it full of the thoughts it speaks: but if you ask it something that you want to know about what is said, it looks at you always with the same one sign. And, once committed to writing, discourse is tossed about everywhere indiscriminately, among those who understand and those to whom it is naught, and who cannot select the fit from the unfit." Plato further complains, adds Mr. Martineau, that "Theuth, the inventor of letters, had ruined men's memories and living command of their knowledge, by inducing a lazy trust in records ready to their hand: and he limits the benefit of the litera scripta to the compensation it provides for the failing memory of old age, when reading naturally becomes the great solace of life.... Plato's tone is invariably depreciatory of everything committed to writing, with the exception of laws."

This was also the early Rabbinical view, for while the Law might, nay, must, be written, the rest of the tradition was to be orally confided. The oral book was the specialty of the Rabbinical schools. We moderns, who are to the ancients, in Rabbinic phrase, as asses to angels in intellect, cannot rely upon oral teaching–our memory is too weak to bear the strain. Even when a student attends an oral lecture, he proves my point, because he takes notes.

The ideal lies, as usual, in a compromise. Reading profits most when, beside the book, you have some one with whom to talk about the book. If that some one be the author of the book, good; if it be your teacher, better; if it be a fellow-student, better still; if it be members of your family circle, best of all. The teacher has only succeeded when he feels that his students can do without him, can use their books by themselves and for themselves. But personal intercourse in studies between equals is never obsolete. "Provide thyself with a fellow-student," said the Rabbi. Friendship made over a book is fast, enduring; this friendship is the great solace. How much we Jews have lost in modern times in having given up the old habit of reading good books together in the family circle! Religious literature thus had a halo of home about it, and the halo never faded throughout life. From the pages of the book in after years the father's loving voice still spoke to his child. But when it comes to the author, I have doubts whether it be at all good to have him near you when you read his book. You may take an unfair advantage of him, and reject his book, because you find the writer personally antipathetic. Or he may take an unfair advantage of you, and control you by his personal fascination. You remember the critic of Demosthenes, who remarked to him of a certain oration, "When I first read your speech, I was convinced, just as the Athenians were; but when I read it again, I saw through its fallacies." "Yes," rejoined Demosthenes, "but the Athenians heard it only once." A book you read more than once: for you possess only what you understand. I do not doubt that the best readers are those who move least in literary circles, who are unprejudiced one way or the other by their personal likes or dislikes of literary men. How detestable are personal paragraphs about authors–often, alas! autobiographical titbits. We expect a little more reticence: we expect the author to say what he has to say in his book, and not in his talks about his book and himself. We expect him to express himself and suppress himself. "Respect the books," says Judah the Pious, "or you show disrespect to the writer." No, not to the writer, but to the soul whose progeny the book is, to the living intellect that bred it, in Milton's noble phrase, to "an Immortality rather than a life." "Many a man," he says, "lives a burden to the earth; but a good book is the precious life-blood of a master-spirit, embalmed and treasured up on purpose to a life beyond life."

It is a sober truth that, of the books we chiefly love, we know least about the authors. Perpetrating probably the only joke in his great Bodleian Catalogue, Dr. Steinschneider enters the Bible under the heading Anonyma. We are nowadays so concerned to know whether Moses or another wrote the Pentateuch, that we neglect the Pentateuch as though no one had ever written it. What do we know about the personality of Shakespeare? Perhaps we are happy in our ignorance. "Sometimes," said Jonathan Swift, "I read a book with pleasure and detest the author." Most of us would say the same of Jonathan Swift himself, and all of us, I think, share R.L. Stevenson's resentment against a book with the portrait of a living author, and in a heightened degree against an English translation of an ancient Hebrew classic with the translator's portrait. Sometimes such a translator is the author; his rendering, at all events, is not the classic. A certain Fidentinus once stole the work of the Roman poet Martial, and read it out to the assembly as his own; whereupon Martial wrote this epigram,

> The book you read is, Fidentinus, mine,
>
> Tho' read so badly, it well may pass for thine.

But even apart from such bad taste as the aforementioned translator's, I do not like to see portraits of living authors in their books. The author of a good book becomes your intimate, but it is the author as you know him from his book, not as you see him in the flesh or on a silver print. I quote Stevenson again: "When you have read, you carry away with you a memory of the man himself; it is as though you had touched a loyal hand, looked into brave eyes, and made a noble friend; there is another bond on you thenceforward, binding you to life and to the love of virtue."

This line of thought leads me to the further remark, that some part of the solace derived from books has changed its character since the art of printing was invented. In former times the personality, if not of the author, at all events of the scribe, pressed itself perforce upon the reader. The reader had before him, not necessarily an autograph, but at all events a manuscript. Printing has suppressed this individuality, and the change is not all for the better. The evil consists in this, that whereas of old a book, being handwritten, was clearly recognized as the work of some one's hand, it now assumes, being printed, an impersonal importance, which may be beyond its deserts. Especially is this the case with what we may term religious authorities; we are now apt to forget that behind the authority there stands simply–the author. It is instructive to contrast the customary method of citing two great codifiers of Jewish law–Maimonides and Joseph Caro. Caro lived in the age of printing, and the Shulchan Aruch was the first great Jewish book composed after the printing-press was in operation. The result has been, that the Shulchan Aruch has become an impersonal authority, rarely cited by the author's name, while the Mishneh Torah is mostly referred to as the Rambam, i.e. Maimonides.

For all that, printing has been a gain, even from the point of view at which I have just arrived. Not only has it demolished the barrier which the scribe's personality interposed between author and reader, but, by increasing the number of readers, it has added to the solace of each. For the solace of books is never selfish–the book-miser is never the book-lover, nor does the mere collector of rarities and preciosities deserve that name, for the one hoards, but does not own; the other serves Mammon, not God. The modern cheapening of books–the immediate result of printing–not only extends culture, it intensifies culture. Your joy in a book is truest when the book is cheapest, when you know that it is, or might be, in the hands of thousands of others, who go with you in the throng towards the same divine joy.

These sentiments are clearly those of a Philistine. The fate of that last word, by the way, is curious. The Philistines, Mr. Macalister discovered when excavating Gezer, were the only artistic people in Palestine! Using the term, however, in the sense to which Matthew Arnold gave vogue, I am a Philistine in taste, I suppose, for I never can bring myself nowadays to buy a second-hand book. For dusty old tomes, I go to the public library; but my own private books must be sweet and clean. There are many who prefer old copies, who revel in the inscribed names of former owners, and prize their marginal annotations. If there be some special sentimental associations connected with these factors, if the books be heirlooms, and the annotations come from a vanished, but beloved, hand, then the old book becomes an old love. But in most cases these things seem to me the defects of youth, not the virtues of age; for they are usually too recent to be venerable, though they are just old enough to disfigure. Let my books be young, fresh, and fragrant in their virgin purity, unspotted from the world. If my copy is to be soiled, I want to do all the soiling myself. It is very different with a manuscript, which cannot be too old or too dowdy. These are its graces. Dr. Neubauer once said to me, "I take no interest in a girl who has seen more than seventeen years, nor in a manuscript that has seen less than seven hundred." Alonzo of Aragon was wont to say in commendation of age, that "age appeared to be best in four things: old wood to burn; old wine to drink; old friends to trust; and old authors to read."

This, however, is not my present point, for I have too much consideration for my readers to attempt to embroil them in the old "battle of the books" that raged round the silly question whether the ancients or the moderns wrote better. I am discussing the age, not of the author, but of the copy. As a critic, as an admirer of old printing, as an archeologist, I feel regard for the editio princeps, but as a lover I prefer the cheap reprint. Old manuscripts certainly have their charm, but they must have been written at least before the invention of printing. Otherwise a manuscript is an anachronism–it recalls too readily the editorial "declined with thanks." At best, the autograph original of a modern work is a literary curiosity, it reveals the author's mechanism, not his mind. But old manuscripts are in a different case; their age has increased their charm, mellowed and confirmed their graces, whether they be canonical books, which "defile the hand" in the Rabbinical sense, or Genizah-grimed fragments, which soil the fingers more literally. And when the dust of ages is removed, these old-world relics renew their youth, and stand forth as witnesses to Israel's unshakable devotion to his heritage.

I have confessed to one Philistine habit; let me plead guilty to another. I prefer to read a book rather than hear a lecture, because in the case of the book I can turn to the last page first. I do like to know before I start whether he marries her in the end or not. You cannot do this with a spoken discourse, for you have to wait the lecturer's pleasure, and may discover to your chagrin, not only that the end is very long in coming, but that when it does come, it is of such a nature that, had you foreseen it, you would certainly not have been present at the beginning. The real interest of a love story is its process: though you may read the consummation first, you are still anxious as to the course of the courtship. But, in sober earnest, those people err who censure readers for trying to peep at the last page first. For this much-abused habit has a deep significance when applied to life. You will remember the ritual rule, "It is the custom of all Israel for the reader of the Scroll of Esther to read and spread out the Scroll like a letter, to make the miracle visible." I remember hearing a sermon just before Purim, in Vienna, and the Jewish preacher gave an admirable homiletic explanation of this rule. He pointed out that in the story of Esther the fate of the Jews has very dark moments, destruction faces them, and hope is remote. But in the end? In the end all goes well. Now, by spreading out the Megillah in folds, displaying the end with the beginning, "the miracle is made visible." Once Lord Salisbury, when some timid Englishmen regarded the approach of the Russians to India as a menace, told his countrymen to use large-scale maps, for these would convince them that the Russians were not so near India after all. We Jews suffer from the same nervousness. We need to use large-scale charts of human history. We need to read history in centuries, not in years. Then we should see things in their true perspective, with God changeless, as men move down the ringing grooves of change. We should then be fuller of content and confidence. We might gain a glimpse of the Divine plan, and might perhaps get out of our habit of crying "All is lost" at every passing persecution. As if never before had there been weeping for a night! As if there had not always been abounding joy the morning after! Then let us, like God Himself, try to see the end in the beginning, let us spread out the Scroll, so that the glory of the finish may transfigure and illumine the gloom and sadness of the intermediate course, and thus "the miracle" of God's providential love will be "made visible" to all who have eyes to see it.

  What strikes a real lover of books when he casts his eye over the fine things that have been said about reading, is this: there is too much said about profit, about advantage. "Reading," said Bacon, "maketh a full man," and reading has been justified a thousand times on this famous plea. But, some one else, I forget who, says, "You may as well expect to become strong by always eating, as wise by always reading." Herbert Spencer was once blamed by a friend for reading so little. Spencer replied, "If I read as much as you do, I should know as little as you do." Too many of the eulogies of books are utilitarian. A book has been termed "the home traveller's ship or horse," and libraries, "the wardrobes of literature." Another favorite phrase is Montaigne's, "'Tis the best viaticum for this human journey," a phrase paralleled by the Rabbinic use of the Biblical "provender for the way." "The aliment of youth, the comfort of old age," so Cicero terms books. "The sick man is not to be pitied when he has his cure in his sleeve"–that is where they used to carry their books. But I cannot go through the long list of the beautiful, yet inadequate, similes that abound in the works of great men, many of which can be read in the "Book-Lover's Enchiridion," to which I have already alluded.

    One constant comparison is of books to friends. This is perhaps best worked out in one of the Epistles of Erasmus, which the "Enchiridion" omits: "You want to know what I am doing. I devote myself to my friends, with whom I enjoy the most delightful intercourse. With them I shut myself in some corner, where I avoid the gaping crowd, and either speak to them in sweet whispers, or listen to their gentle voices, talking with them as with myself. Can anything be more convenient than this? They never hide their own secrets, while they keep sacred whatever is entrusted to them. They speak when bidden, and when not bidden they hold their tongue. They talk of what you wish, and as long as you wish; do not flatter, feign nothing, keep back nothing, freely tell you of your faults, and take no man's character away. What they say is either amusing or wholesome. In prosperity they moderate, in affliction they console; they do not vary with fortune, they follow you in all dangers, and last out to the very grave. Nothing can be more candid than their relations with one another. I visit them from time to time, now choosing one companion and now another, with perfect impartiality. With these humble friends, I bury myself in seclusion. What wealth or what sceptres would I take in exchange for this tranquil life?"

    Tranquillity is a not unworthy characteristic of the scholar, but, taking Erasmus at his word, would he not have been even a greater man than he was, had he been less tranquil and more strenuous? His great rôle in the history of European culture would have been greater still, had he been readier to bear the rubs which come from rough contact with the world. I will not, however, allow myself to be led off into this alluring digression, whether books or experience make a man wiser. Books may simply turn a man into a "learned fool," and, on the other hand, experience may equally fail to teach any of the lessons of wisdom. As Moore says:

> My only books
>
> Were woman's looks,
>
> And folly's all they taught me.

The so-called men of the world often know little enough of the world of men. It is a delusion to think that the business man is necessarily business-like. Your business man is often the most un-business-like creature imaginable. For practical ability, give me the man of letters. Life among books often leads to insight into the book of life. At Cambridge we speak of the reading men and the sporting men. Sir Richard Jebb, when he went to Cambridge, was asked, "Do you mean to be a sporting man or a reading man?" He replied, "Neither! I want to be a man who reads." Marcus Aurelius, the scholar and philosopher, was not the least efficient of the Emperors of Rome. James Martineau was right when he said that the student not only becomes a better man, but he also becomes a better student, when he concerns himself with the practical affairs of life as well as with his books. And the idea cuts both ways. We should be better men of business if we were also men of books. It is not necessary to recall that the ancient Rabbis were not professional bookmen. They were smiths and ploughmen, traders and merchants, and their businesses and their trades were idealized and ennobled–and, may we not add, their handiwork improved?–by the expenditure of their leisure in the schools and libraries of Jerusalem.

And so all the foregoing comparisons between books and other objects of utility or delight, charming though some of these comparisons are, fail to satisfy one. One feels that the old Jewish conception is the only completely true one: that conception which came to its climax in the appointment of a benediction to be uttered before beginning to read a book of the Law.

The real solace of books comes from the sense of service, to be rendered or received; and one must enter that holy of holies, the library, with a grateful benediction on one's lip, and humility and reverence and joy in one's soul. Of all the writers about books, Charles Lamb, in his playful way, comes nearest to this old-world, yet imperishable, ideal of the Jewish sages. He says: "I own that I am disposed to say grace upon twenty other occasions in the course of the day besides my dinner. I want a form for setting out on a pleasant walk, for a midnight ramble, for a friendly meeting, for a solved problem. Why have we none for books, those spiritual repasts–a grace before Milton,–a grace before Shakespeare,–a devotional exercise proper to be said before reading the Fairy Queen?" The Jewish ritual could have supplied Lamb with several of these graces.

It will, I hope, now be seen why in speaking on the solace of books I have said so little about consolation. It pains me to hear books praised as a relief from worldly cares, to hear the library likened to an asylum for broken spirits. I have never been an admirer of Boëthius. His "Consolations of Philosophy" have always been influential and popular, but I like better the first famous English translator than the original Latin author. Boëthius wrote in the sixth century as a fallen man, as one to whom philosophy came in lieu of the mundane glory which he had once possessed, and had now lost. But Alfred the Great turned the "Consolations" into English at the moment of his greatest power. He translated it in the year 886, when king on a secure throne; in his brightest days, when the Danish clouds had cleared. Sorrow has often produced great books, great psalms, to which the sorrowful heart turns for solace. But in the truest sense the Shechinah rests on man only in his joy, when he has so attuned his life that misfortune is but another name for good fortune. He must have learned to endure before he seeks the solace of communion with the souls of the great, with the soul of God. Very saddening it is to note how often men have turned to books because life has no other good. The real book-lover goes to his books when life is fullest of other joys, when his life is richest in its manifold happiness. Then he adds the crown of joy to his other joys, and finds the highest happiness.

I do not like to think of the circumstances under which Sir Thomas Bodley went to Oxford to found his famous library. Not till his diplomatic career was a failure, not till Elizabeth's smiles had darkened into frowns, did he set up his staff at the library door. But Bodley rather mistook himself. As a lad the library had been his joy, and when he was abroad, at the summit of his public fame, he turned his diplomatic missions to account by collecting books and laying the foundation of his future munificence. I even think that no lover of books ever loved them so well in his adversity as in his prosperity. Another view was held by Don Isaac Abarbanel, the famous Jewish statesman and litterateur. Under Alfonso V, of Portugal, and other rulers, he attained high place, but was brought low by the Inquisition, and shared in the expulsion of his brethren. He writes in one of his letters: "The whole time I lived in the courts and palaces of kings, occupied in their service, I had no leisure to read or write books. My days were spent in vain ambitions, seeking after wealth and honor. Now that my wealth is gone, and honor has become exiled from Israel; now that I am a vagabond and a wanderer on the earth, and I have no money: now, I have returned to seek the book of God, as it is said, [Hebrew: cheth-samech-vav-resh-yod mem-cheth-samech-resh-aleph vav-hey-chaf-yod qof-tav-nun-yod], 'He is in sore need, therefore he studies.'"

This is witty, but it is not wise. Fortunately, it is not quite true; Abarbanel does little justice to himself in this passage, for elsewhere (in the preface to his Commentary on Kings) he draws a very different picture of his life in his brilliant court days. "My house," he says, "was an assembly place for the wise ... in my abode and within my walls were wealth and fame for the Torah and for those made great in its lore." Naturally, the active statesman had less leisure for his books than the exiled, fallen minister.

So, too, with an earlier Jewish writer, Saadia. No sadder title was ever chosen for a work than his Sefer ha-Galui–"Book of the Exiled." It is beyond our province to enter into his career, full of stress and storm. Between 933 and 937, driven from power, he retired to his library at Bagdad, just as Cincinnatus withdrew to his farm when Rome no longer needed him. During his retirement Saadia's best books were written. Why? Graetz tells us that "Saadia was still under the ban of excommunication. He had, therefore, no other sphere of action than that of an author." This is pitiful; but, again, it is not altogether true. Saadia's whole career was that of active authorship, when in power and out of power, as a boy, in middle life, in age: his constant thought was the service of truth, in so far as literature can serve it, and one may well think that he felt that the Crown of the Law was better worth wearing in prosperity, when he chose it out of other crowns, than in adversity, when it was the only crown within his reach. It was thus that King Solomon chose.

So, in speaking of the solace of books, I have ventured to employ "solace" in an old, unusual sense. "Solace" has many meanings. It means "comfort in sorrow," and in Scotch law it denotes a compensation for wounded feelings, solatium, moral and intellectual damages in short. But in Chaucer and Spenser, "solace" is sometimes used as a synonym for joy and sweet exhilaration. This is an obsolete use, but let me hope that the thing is not obsolete. For one must go to his books for solace, not in mourning garb, but in gayest attire–to a wedding, not to a funeral. When John Clare wrote,

> I read in books for happiness,
> But books mistake the way to joy,

he read for what he ought to have brought, and thus he failed to find his goal. The library has been beautifully termed the "bridal chamber of the mind." So, too, the Apocrypha puts it in the Wisdom of Solomon:

Wisdom is radiant....
Her I loved and sought out from my youth,
And I sought to take her for my bride,
And I became enamored of her beauty.

* * * * *

When I am come into my house, I shall find rest with her,
For converse with her hath no bitterness,
And to live with her hath no pain.

* * * * *

O God of the fathers, ...
Give me wisdom, that sitteth by Thee on Thy throne.

Medieval Wayfaring

Men leave their homes because they must, or because they will. The Hebrew has experienced both motives for travelling. Irresistibly driven on by his own destiny and by the pressure of his fellow-men, the Jew was also gifted with a double share of that curiosity and restlessness which often send men forth of their own free will on long and arduous journeys. He has thus played the part of the Wandering Jew from choice and from necessity. He loved to live in the whole world, and the whole world met him by refusing him a single spot that he might call his very own.

> Tribes of the wandering foot and weary breast,
> How shall ye flee away and be at rest!
> The wild-dove hath her nest, the fox her cave,
> Mankind their country,–Israel but the grave!

A sad chapter of medieval history is filled with the enforced wanderings of the sons of Israel. The lawgiver prophesied well, "There shall be no rest for the sole of thy foot." But we are not concerned here with the victim of expulsion and persecution. The wayfarer with whom we shall deal is the traveller, and not the exile. He was moved by no caprice but his own. He will excite our admiration, perhaps our sympathy, only rarely our tears.

My subject, be it remembered, is not wayfarers, but wayfaring. Hence I am to tell you not the story of particular travellers, but the manner of their travelling, the conditions under which they moved. Before leaving home, a Jewish wayfarer of the Middle Ages was bound to procure two kinds of passport. In no country in those days was freedom of motion allowed to anyone. The Jew was simply a little more hampered than others. In England, the Jew paid a feudal fine before he might cross the seas. In Spain, the system of exactions was very complete. No Jew could change his residence without a license even within his own town. But in addition to the inflictions of the Government, the Jews enacted voluntary laws of their own, forcing their brethren to obtain a congregational permit before starting.

The reasons for this restriction were simple. In the first place, no Jew could be allowed to depart at will, and leave the whole burden of the royal taxes on the shoulders of those who were left behind. Hence, in many parts of Europe and Asia, no Jew could leave without the express consent of the congregation. Even when he received the consent, it was usually on the understanding that he would continue, in his absence, to pay his share of the communal dues. Sometimes even women were included in this law, as, for instance, if the daughter of a resident Jew married and settled elsewhere, she was forced to contribute to the taxes of her native town a sum proportionate to her dowry, unless she emigrated to Palestine, in which case she was free. A further cause why Jews placed restrictions on free movement was moral and commercial. Announcements had to be made in the synagogue informing the congregation that so-and-so was on the point of departure, and anyone with claims against him could obtain satisfaction. No clandestine or unauthorized departure was permissible. It must not be thought that these communal licenses were of no service to the traveller. On the contrary, they often assured him a welcome in the next town, and in Persia were as good as a safe-conduct. No Mohammedan would have dared defy the travelling order sealed by the Jewish Patriarch.

Having obtained his two licenses, one from the Government and the other from the Synagogue, the traveller would have to consider his costume. "Dress shabbily" was the general Jewish maxim for the tourist. How necessary this rule was, may be seen from what happened to Rabbi Petachiah, who travelled from Prague to Nineveh, in 1175, or thereabouts. At Nineveh he fell sick, and the king's physicians attended him and pronounced his death certain. Now Petachiah had travelled in most costly attire, and in Persia the rule was that if a Jewish traveller died, the physicians took half his property. Petachiah saw through the real danger that threatened him, so he escaped from the perilous ministrations of the royal doctors, had himself carried across the Tigris on a raft, and soon recovered. Clearly, it was imprudent of a Jewish traveller to excite the rapacity of kings or bandits by wearing rich dresses. But it was also desirable for the Jew, if he could, to evade recognition as such altogether. Jewish opinion was very sensible on this head. It did not forbid a Jew's disguising himself even as a priest of the Church, joining a caravan, and mumbling Latin hymns. In times of danger, he might, to save his life, don the turban and pass as a Mohammedan even in his home. Most remarkable concession of all, the Jewess on a journey might wear the dress of a man. The law of the land was equally open to reason. In Spain, the Jew was allowed to discard his yellow badge while travelling; in Germany, he had the same privilege, but he had to pay a premium for it. In some parts, the Jewish community as a whole bought the right to travel and to discard the badge on journeys, paying a lump sum for the general privilege, and itself exacting a communal tax to defray the general cost. In Rome, the traveller was allowed to lodge for ten days before resuming his hated badge. But, curiously enough, the legal relaxation concerning the badge was not extended to the markets. The Jew made the medieval markets, yet he was treated as an unwelcome guest, a commodity to be taxed. This was especially so in Germany. In 1226, Bishop Lorenz, of Breslau, ordered Jews who passed through his domain to pay the same toll as slaves brought to market. The visiting Jew paid toll for everything; but he got part of his money back. He received a yellow badge, which he was forced to wear during his whole stay at the market, the finances of which he enriched, indirectly by his trade, and directly by his huge contributions to the local taxes.

The Jewish traveller mostly left his wife at home. In certain circumstances he could force her to go with him, as, for instance, if he had resolved to settle in Palestine. On the other hand, the wife could prevent her husband from leaving her during the first year after marriage. It also happened that families emigrated together. Mostly, however, the Jewess remained at home, and only rarely did she join even the pilgrimage to Jerusalem. This is a striking contrast to the Christian custom, for it was the Christian woman that was the most ardent pilgrim; in fact, pilgrimages to the Holy Land only became popular in Church circles because of the enthusiasm of Helena, mother of Constantine the Great, especially when, in 326, she found the true cross. We, however, read of an aged Jewess who made a pilgrimage to all the cities of Europe, for the purpose of praying in the synagogues on her route.

We now know, from the Chronicle of Achimaaz, that Jews visited Jerusalem in the tenth century. Aronius records a curious incident. Charles the Great, between the years 787 and 813, ordered a Jewish merchant, who often used to visit Palestine and bring precious and unknown commodities thence to the West, to hoax the Archbishop of Mainz, so as to lower the self-conceit of this vain dilettante. The Jew thereupon sold him a mouse at a high price, persuading him that it was a rare animal, which he had brought with him from Judea. Early in the eleventh century there was a fully organized Jewish community with a Beth-Din at Ramleh, some four hours' drive from Jaffa. But Jews did not visit Palestine in large numbers, until Saladin finally regained the Holy City for Mohammedan rule, towards the end of the twelfth century. From that time pilgrimages of Jews became more frequent; but the real influx of Jews into Palestine dates from 1492, when many of the Spanish exiles settled there, and formed the nucleus of the present Sefardic population.

On the whole, it may be said that in the Middle Ages the journey to Palestine was fraught with so much danger that it was gallantry that induced men to go mostly without their wives. And, generally speaking, the Jew going abroad to earn a living for his family, could not dream of allowing his wife to share the dangers and fatigues of the way. In Ellul, 1146, Rabbi Simeon the Pious returned from England, where he had lived many years, and betook himself to Cologne, thence to take ship home to Trier. On the way, near Cologne, he was slain by Crusaders, because he refused baptism. The Jewish community of Cologne bought the body from the citizens, and buried it in the Jewish cemetery.

No doubt it was often a cruel necessity that separated husband and wife. The Jewish law, even in lands where monogamy was not legally enforced, did not allow the Jew, however, to console himself with one wife at home and another abroad. Josephus, we know, had one wife in Tiberias and another in Alexandria, and the same thing is told us of royal officers in the Roman period; but the Talmudic legislation absolutely forbids such license, even though it did not formally prohibit a man from having more than one wife at home. We hear occasionally of the wife's growing restive in her husband's absence and taking another husband. In 1272, Isaac of Erfurt went on a trading journey, and though he was only gone from March 9, 1271, to July,

1272, he found, on his return, that his wife had wearied of waiting for him. Such incidents on the side of the wife were very rare; the number of cases in which wife-desertion occurred was larger. In her husband's absence, the wife's lot, at best, was not happy. "Come back," wrote one wife, "or send me a divorce." "Nay," replied the husband, "I can do neither. I have not yet made enough provision for us, so I cannot return. And, before Heaven, I love you, so I cannot divorce you." The Rabbi advised that he should give her a conditional divorce, a kindly device, which provided that, in case the husband remained away beyond a fixed date, the wife was free to make other matrimonial arrangements. The Rabbis held that travelling diminishes family life, property, and reputation. Move from house to house, and you lose a shirt; go from place to place, and you lose a life–so ran the Rabbinic proverb. This subject might be enlarged upon, but enough has been said to show that this breaking up of the family life was one of the worst effects of the Jewish travels of the Middle Ages, and even more recent times.

Whether his journey was devotional or commercial, the rites of religion formed part of the traveller's preparations for the start. The Prayer for Wayfarers is Talmudic in origin. It may be found in many prayer books, and I need not quote it. But one part of it puts so well, in a few pregnant words, the whole story of danger, that I must reproduce them. On approaching a town, the Jew prayed, "May it be Thy will, O Lord, to bring me safely to this town." When he had entered, he prayed, "May it be Thy will, O Lord, to take me safely from this town." And when he actually left, he uttered similar words, pathetic and painfully significant.

In the first century of the Christian era, much travelling was entailed by the conveyance of the didrachmon, sent by each Jew to the Temple from almost every part of the known world. Philo says of the Jews beyond the Euphrates: "Every year the sacred messengers are sent to convey large sums of gold and silver to the Temple, which have been collected from all the subordinate Governments. They travel over rugged and difficult and almost impassable roads, which, however, they look upon as level and easy, inasmuch as they serve to conduct them to piety." And the road was made easy in other ways.

It must often have been shortened to the imagination by the prevalent belief that by supernatural aid the miles could be actually lessened. Rabbi Natronai was reported to be able to convey himself a several days' journey in a single instant. So Benjamin of Tudela tells how Alroy, who claimed to be the Messiah in the twelfth century, not only could make himself visible or invisible at will, but could cross rivers on his turban, and, by the aid of the Divine Name, could travel a ten days' journey in ten hours. Another Jewish traveller calmed the sea by naming God, another by writing the sacred Name on a shard, and casting it into the sea. "Have no care," said he, on another occasion, to his Arab comrade, as the shadows fell on a Friday afternoon, and they were still far from home, "have no care, we shall arrive before nightfall," and, exercising his wonderworking powers, he was as good as his word. We read in Achimaaz of the exploits of a tenth-century Jew who traversed Italy, working wonders, being received everywhere with popular acclamations. This was Aaron of Bagdad, son of a miller, who, finding that a lion had eaten the mill-mule, caught the lion and made him do the grinding. His father sent him on his travels as a penalty for his dealings with magic: after three years he might return. Fie went on board a ship, and assured the sailors that they need fear neither foe nor storm, for he could use the Name. He landed at Gaeta in Italy, where he restored to human form the son of his host, whom a witch had turned into an ass. This was the beginning of many miracles. But he did not allow one place to monopolize him. Next we find him in Benvenuto. He goes to the synagogue, recognizes that a lad omits the name of God from his prayer, thus showing that he is dead! He goes to Oria, then to Bari, and so forth. Similar marvels were told in the Midrash, of travellers like Father Jacob, and in the lives of Christian saints.

But the Jew had a real means of shortening the way–by profitable and edifying conversation. "Do not travel with an Am ha-Arez," the olden Rabbis advised. Such a one, they held, was careless of his own safety, and would hardly be more careful of his companion's life. But, besides, an Am ha-Arez, using the word in its later sense of ignoramus, would be too dull for edifying conversation, and one might as well or as ill journey alone as with a boor. But "thou shalt speak of them by the way," says Deuteronomy of the commandments, and this (to say nothing of the danger) was one of the reasons why solitary travelling was disapproved. A man walking alone was more likely to turn his mind to idle thoughts, than if he had a congenial partner to converse with, and the Mishnah is severe against him who turns aside from his peripatetic study to admire a tree or a fallow. This does not imply that the Jews were indifferent to the beauties of nature. Jewish travellers often describe the scenery of the parts they visit, and Petachiah literally revels in the beautiful gardens of Persia, which he paints in vivid colors. Then, again, few better descriptions of a storm at sea have been written than those composed by Jehudah Halevi on his fatal voyage to Palestine. Similarly, Charizi, another Jewish wayfarer, who laughed himself over half the world, wrote verses as he walked, to relieve the tedium. He is perhaps the most entertaining of all Jewish travellers. Nothing is more amusing than his conscious habit of judging the characters of the men he saw by their hospitality, or the reverse, to himself. A more serious traveller, Maimonides, must have done a good deal of thinking on horseback, to get through his ordinary day's work and write his great books. In fact, he himself informs us that he composed part of his Commentary to the Mishnah while journeying by land and sea. In Europe, the Rabbis often had several neighboring congregations under their care, and on their journeys to and fro took their books with them, and read in them at intervals. Maharil, on such journeys, always took note of the Jewish customs observed in different localities. He was also a most skilful and successful Shadchan, or marriage-broker, and his extensive travels placed this famous Rabbi in an excellent position for match-making. Certainly, the marriages he effected were notoriously prosperous, and in his hands the Shadchan system did the most good and the least harm of which it is capable.

Another type of short-distance traveller was the Bachur, or student. Not that his journeys were always short, but he rarely crossed the sea. In the second century we find Jewish students in Galilee behaving as many Scotch youths did before the days of Carnegie funds. These students would study in Sepphoris in the winter, and work in the fields in summer. After the impoverishment caused by the Bar-Cochba war, the students were glad to dine at the table of the wealthy Patriarch Judah I. In the medieval period there were also such. These Bachurim, who, young as they were, were often married, accomplished enormous journeys on foot. They walked from the Rhine to Vienna, and from North Germany to Italy. Their privations on the road were indescribable. Bad weather was naturally a severe trial. "Hearken not to the prayers of wayfarers," was the petition of those who stayed at home. This quaint Talmudic saying refers to the selfishness of travellers, who always clamor for fine weather, though the farmer needs rain. Apart from the weather, the Bachurim suffered much on the road. Their ordinary food was raw vegetables culled from the fields; they drank nothing but water. They were often accompanied by their teachers, who underwent the same privations. Unlike their Talmudical precursors, they travelled much by night, because it was safer, and also because they reserved the daylight for study. The dietary laws make Jewish travelling particularly irksome. We do, indeed, find Jews lodging at the ordinary inns, but they could not join the general company at the table d'hôte. The Sabbath, too, was the cause of some discomfort, though the traveller always exerted his utmost efforts to reach a Jewish congregation by Friday evening, sometimes, as we have seen, with supernatural aid.

We must interrupt this account of the Bachur to record a much earlier instance of the awkward situation in which a pious Jewish traveller might find himself because of the Sabbath regulations. In the very last year of the fourth century, Synesius, of Cyrene, writing to his brother of his voyage from Alexandria to Constantinople, supplies us with a quaint instance of the manner in which the Sabbath affected Jewish travellers. Synesius uses a sarcastic tone, which must not be taken as seriously unfriendly. "His voyage homeward," says Mr. Glover, "was adventurous." It is a pity that space cannot be found for a full citation of Synesius's enthralling narrative. His Jewish steersman is an entertaining character. There were twelve members in the crew, the steersman making the thirteenth. More than half, including the steersman, were Jews. "It was," says Synesius, "the day which the Jews call the Preparation [Friday], and they reckon the night to the next day, on which they are not allowed to do any work, but they pay it especial honor, and rest on it. So the steersman let go the helm from his hands, when he thought the sun would have set on the land, and threw himself down, and 'What mariner should choose might trample him!' We did not at first understand the real reason, but took it for despair, and went to him and besought him not to give up all hope yet. For in plain fact the big rollers still kept on, and the sea was at issue with itself. It does this when the wind falls, and the waves it has set going do not fall with it, but, still retaining in full force the impulse that started them, meet the onset of the gale, and to its front oppose their own. Well, when people are sailing in such circumstances, life hangs, as they say, by a slender thread. But if the steersman is a Rabbi into the bargain, what are one's feelings? When, then, we understood what he meant in leaving the helm,–for when we begged him to save the ship from danger, he went on reading his book,–we despaired of persuasion, and tried force. And a gallant soldier (for we have with us a good few Arabians, who belong to the cavalry) drew his sword, and threatened to cut his head off, if he would not steer the ship. But in a moment he was a genuine Maccabee, and would stick to his dogma. Yet when it was now midnight, he took his place of his own accord, 'for now,' says he, 'the law allows me, as we are clearly in danger of our lives.' At that the tumult begins again, moaning of men and screaming of women. Everybody began calling on Heaven, and wailing and remembering their dear ones. Amarantus alone was cheerful, thinking he was on the point of ruling out his creditors." Amarantus was the captain, who wished to die, because he was deep in debt. What with the devil-may-care captain, the Maccabean steersman, and the critical onlooker, who was a devoted admirer of Hypatia, rarely has wayfaring been conducted under more delightful conditions. As is often the case in life, the humors of the scene almost obscure the fact that the lives of the actors were in real danger. But all ended well. "As for us," says Synesius further on, "as soon as we reached the land we longed for, we embraced it as if it had been a living mother. Offering, as usual, a hymn of gratitude to God, I added to it the recent misadventure from which we had unexpectedly been saved."

   To return to our travelling Bachur of later centuries than Synesius's Rabbi-steersman. On the road, the student was often attacked, but, as happened with the son of the great Asheri, who was waylaid by bandits near Toledo, the robbers did not always get the best of the fight. The Bachur could take his own part. One Jew gained much notoriety in 801 by conducting an elephant all the way from Haroun al-Rashid's court as a present to

Charlemagne, the king of the Franks. But the Rabbi suffered considerably from his religion on his journeys. Dr. Schechter tells us how the Gaon Elijah got out of his carriage to say his prayer, and, as the driver knew that the Rabbi would not interrupt his devotions, he promptly made off, carrying away the Gaon's property.

But the account was not all on one side. If the Bachur suffered for his religion, he received ample compensation. When he arrived at his destination, he was welcomed right heartily. We read how cordially the Sheliach Kolel was received in Algiers in the fifteenth to eighteenth centuries. It was a great popular event, as is nowadays the visit of the Alliance inspector. This was not the case with all Jewish travellers, some of whom received a very cold shoulder from their brethren. Why was this? Chiefly because the Jews, as little as the rest of medieval peoples, realized that progress and enlightenment are indissolubly bound up with the right of free movement. They regarded the right to move here and there at will as a selfish privilege of the few, not the just right of all. But more than that. The Jews were forced to live in special and limited Ghettos. It was not easy to find room for newcomers. When a crisis arrived, such as the expulsion of the Jews from Spain, then, except here and there, the Jews were generous to a fault in providing for the exiles. Societies all over the Continent and round the coast of the Mediterranean spent their time and money in ransoming the poor victims, who, driven from Spain, were enslaved by the captains of the vessels that carried them, and were then bought back to freedom by their Jewish brethren.

This is a noble fact in Jewish history. But it is nevertheless true that Jewish communities were reluctant in ordinary times to permit new settlements. This was not so in ancient times. Among the Essenes, a newcomer had a perfectly equal right to share everything with the old inhabitants. These Essenes were great travellers, going from city to city, probably with propagandist aims. In the Talmudic law there are very clear rules on the subject of passers through a town or immigrants into it. By that law persons staying in a place for less than thirty days were free from all local dues except special collections for the poor. He who stayed less than a year contributed to the ordinary poor relief, but was not taxed for permanent objects, such as walling the town, defences, etc., nor did he contribute to the salaries of teachers and officials, nor the building and support of synagogues. But as his duties were small, so were his rights. After a twelve months' stay he became a "son of the city," a full member of the community. But in the Middle Ages, newcomers, as already said, were not generally welcome. The question of space was one important reason, for all newcomers had to stay in the Ghetto. Secondly, the newcomer was not amenable to discipline. Local custom varied much in the details both of Jewish and general law. The new settler might claim to retain his old customs, and the regard for local custom was so strong that the claim was often allowed, to the destruction of uniformity and the undermining of authority. To give an instance or two: A newcomer would insist that, as he might play cards in his native town, he ought not to be expected to obey puritanical restrictions in the place to which he came. The result was that the resident Jews would clamor against foreigners enjoying special privileges, as in this way all attempts to control gambling might be defeated. Or the newcomer would claim to shave his beard in accordance with his home custom, but to the scandal of the town which he was visiting. The native young men would imitate the foreigner, and then there would be trouble. Or the settler would assert his right to wear colors and fashions and jewelry forbidden to native Jews. Again, the marriage problem was complicated by the arrival of insinuating strangers, who turned out to be married men masquerading as bachelors. Then as to public worship–the congregation was often split into fragments by the independent services organized by foreign groups, and it would become necessary to prohibit its own members from attending the synagogues of foreign settlers. Then as to communal taxes: these were fixed annually on the basis of the population, and the arrival of newcomers seriously disturbed the equilibrium, led to fresh exactions by the Government, which it was by no means certain the new settlers could or would pay, and which, therefore, fell on the shoulders of the old residents.

When we consider all these facts, we can see that the eagerness of the medieval Jews to control the influx of foreign settlers was only in part the result of base motives. And, of course, the exclusion was not permanent or rigid. In Rome, the Sefardic and the Italian Jews fraternally placed their synagogues on different floors of the same building. In some German towns, the foreign synagogue was fixed in the same courtyard as the native.

Everywhere foreign Jews abounded, and everywhere a generous welcome awaited the genuine traveller.

As to the travelling beggar, he was a perpetual nuisance. Yet he was treated with much consideration. The policy with regard to him was, "Send the beggar further," and this suited the tramp, too. He did not wish to settle, he wished to move on. He would be lodged for two days in the communal inn, or if, as usually happened, he arrived on Friday evening, he would be billeted on some hospitable member, or the Shamash would look after him at the public expense. It is not till the thirteenth century that we meet regular envoys sent from Palestine to collect money.

The genuine traveller, however, was an ever-welcome guest. If he came at fair time, his way was smoothed for him. The Jew who visited the fair was only rarely charged local taxes by the Synagogue. He deserved a welcome, for he not only brought wares to sell, but he came laden with new books. The fair was the only book-market At other times the Jews were dependent on the casual visits of travelling venders of volumes. Book-selling does not seem to have been a settled occupation in the Middle Ages. The merchant who came to the fair also fulfilled another function–that of Shadchan. The day of the fair was, in fact, the crisis of the year. Naturally, the letter-carrier was eagerly received. In the early part of the eighteenth century the function of conveying the post was sometimes filled by Jewesses.

Even the ordinary traveller, who had no business to transact, would often choose fair time for visiting new places, for he would be sure to meet interesting people then. He, too, would mostly arrive on a Friday evening, and would beguile the Sabbath with reports of the wonders he had seen. In the great synagogue of Sepphoris, Jochanan was discoursing of the great pearl, so gigantic in size that the Eastern gates of the Temple were to be built of the single gem. "Ay, ay," assented an auditor, who had been a notorious skeptic until he had become a shipwrecked sailor, "had not mine own eyes beheld such a pearl in the ocean-bed, I should not have believed it." And so the medieval traveller would tell his enthralling tales. He would speak of a mighty Jewish kingdom in the East, existing in idyllic peace and prosperity; he would excite his auditors with news of the latest Messiah; he would describe the river Sambatyon, which keeps the Sabbath, and, mingling truth with fiction, with one breath would truly relate how he crossed a river on an inflated skin, and with the next breath romance about Hillel's tomb, how he had been there, and how he had seen a large hollow stone, which remains empty if a bad fellow enters, but at the approach of a pious visitor fills up with sweet, pure water, with which he washes, uttering a wish at the same time, sure that it will come true. It is impossible even to hint at all the wonders of the tombs. Jews were ardent believers in the supernatural power of sepulchres; they made pilgrimages to them to pray and to beg favors. Jewish travellers' tales of the Middle Ages are heavily laden with these legends. Of course, the traveller would also bring genuine news about his brethren in distant parts, and sober information about foreign countries, their ways, their physical conformation, and their strange birds and beasts. These stories were in the main true. For instance, Petachiah tells of a flying camel, which runs fifteen times as fast as the fleetest horse. He must have seen an ostrich, which is still called the flying camel by Arabs. But we cannot linger over this matter. Suffice it to say that, as soon as Sabbath was over, the traveller's narrative would be written out by the local scribe, and treasured as one of the communal prizes. The traveller, on his part, often kept a diary, and himself compiled a description of his adventures. In some congregations there was kept a Communal Note-Book, in which were entered decisions brought by visiting Rabbis from other communities.

The most welcome of guests, even more welcome than long-distance travellers, or globe-trotters, were the Bachurim and travelling Rabbis. The Talmudic Rabbis were most of them travellers. Akiba's extensive journeys were, some think, designed to rouse the Jews of Asia Minor generally to participate in the insurrection against Hadrian. But my narrative must be at this point confined to the medieval students. For the Bachurim, or students, there was a special house in many communities, and they lived together with their teachers. In the twelfth century, the great academy of Narbonne, under Abraham ibn Daud, attracted crowds of foreign students. These, as Benjamin of Tudela tells us, were fed and clothed at the communal cost. At Beaucaire, the students were housed and supported at the teacher's expense. In the seventeenth century, the students not only were paid small bursaries, but every household entertained one or more of them at table. In these circumstances their life was by no means dull or monotonous. A Jewish student endures much, but he knows how to get the best out of life. This optimism, this quickness of humor, saved the Rabbi and his pupil from many a melancholy hour. Take Abraham ibn Ezra, for instance. If ever a man was marked out to be a bitter reviler of fate, it was he. But he laughed at fate. He gaily wandered from his native Spain over many lands penniless, travelled with no baggage but his thoughts, visited Italy and France, and even reached London, where, perhaps, he died. Fortune ill-treated him, but he found many joys. Wherever he went, patrons held out their hand.

Travelling students found many such generous lovers of learning, who, with their wealth, encouraged their guests to write original works or copy out older books, which the patrons then passed on to poor scholars in want of a library. The legend is told, how the prophet Elijah visited Hebron, and was not "called up" in the synagogue. Receiving no Aliyah on earth, he returned to his elevation in Heaven. It was thus imprudent to deny honor to angels unawares. Usually the scholar was treated as such a possible angel. When he arrived, the whole congregation would turn out to meet him. He would be taken in procession to the synagogue, where he would say the benediction ha-Gomel, in thanks for his safety on the road. Perhaps he would address the congregation, though he would do that rather in the school than in the synagogue. Then a banquet would be spread for him. This banquet was called one of the Seudoth Mitzvah, i.e. "commandment meals," to which it was a duty of all pious men to contribute their money and their own attendance. It would be held in the communal hall, used mostly for marriage feasts. When a wedding party came from afar, similar steps for general enjoyment were taken. Men mounted on horseback went forth to welcome the bride, mimic tournaments were fought en route, torch-light processions were made if it were night time, processions by boats if it were in Italy or by the Rhine, a band of communal musicians, retained at general cost, played merry marches, and everyone danced and joined in the choruses. These musicians often went from town to town, and the Jewish players were hired for Gentile parties, just as Jews employed Christian or Arab musicians to help make merry on the Jewish Sabbaths and festivals.

We need not wonder, then, that a traveller like Ibn Ezra was no croaker, but a genial critic of life. He suffered, but he was light-hearted enough to compose witty epigrams and improvise rollicking wine songs. He was an accomplished chess player, and no doubt did something to spread the Eastern game in Europe. Another service rendered by such travellers was the spread of learning by their translations. Their wanderings made them great linguists, and they were thus able to translate medical, astronomical, and scientific works wherever they went. They were also sent by kings on missions to collect new nautical instruments. Thus, the baculus, which helped Columbus to discover America, was taken to Portugal by Jews, and a French Jew was its inventor. They were much in demand as travelling doctors, being summoned from afar to effect specific cures. But they also carried other delights with them. Not only were they among the troubadours, but they were also the most famous of the travelling conteurs. It was the Jews, like Berechiah, Charizi, Zabara, Abraham ibn Chasdai, and other incessant travellers, who helped to bring to Europe Æsop, Bidpai, the Buddhist legends, who "translated them from the Indian," and were partly responsible for this rich poetical gift to the Western world.

Looking back on such a life, Ibn Ezra might well detect a Divine Providence in his own pains and sorrows. So, Jew-like, he retained his hope to the last, and after his buffetings on the troubled seas of life, remembering the beneficent results of his travels to others, if not to himself, he could write in this faithful strain:

> My hope God knoweth well,
> My life He made full sweet;
> Whene'er His servant fell,
> God raised him to his feet.
> Within the garment of His grace,
> My faults He did enfold,
> Hiding my sin, His kindly face
> My God did ne'er withhold.
> Requiting with fresh good,
> My black ingratitude.

There remain the great merchant travellers to be told about. They sailed over all the world, and brought to Europe the wares, the products, the luxuries of the East. They had their own peculiar dangers. Shipwreck was the fate of others besides themselves, but they were peculiarly liable to capture and sale as slaves. Foremost among their more normal hardships I should place the bridge laws of the Middle Ages. The bridges were sometimes practically maintained by the Jewish tolls. In England, before 1290, a Jew paid a toll of a halfpenny on foot and a full penny on horseback–large sums in those days. A "dead Jew" paid eightpence. Burial was for a long time lawful only in London, and the total toll paid for bringing a dead Jew to London over the various bridges must have been considerable. In the Kurpfalz, for instance, the Jewish traveller had to pay the usual "white penny" for every mile, but also a heavy general fee for the whole journey. If he was found without his ticket of leave, he was at once arrested. But it was when he came to a bridge that the exactions grew insufferable. The regulations were somewhat tricky, for the Jew was specially taxed only on Sundays and the Festivals of the Church. But every other day was some Saint's Festival, and while, in Mannheim, even on those days the Christian traveller paid one kreuzer if he crossed the bridge on foot, and two if on horseback, the Jew was charged four kreuzer if on foot, twelve if on a horse, and for every beast of burden he, unlike the Christian wayfarer, paid a further toll of eight kreuzer. The Jewish quarter often lay near the river, and Jews had great occasion for crossing the bridges, even for local needs. In Venice, the Jewish quarter was naturally intersected by bridges; in Rome there was the pons Judeorum, which, no doubt, the Jews had to maintain in repair. It must be remembered that many local Jewish communities paid a regular bridge tax which was not exacted from Christians, and when all this is considered, it will be seen that the Jewish merchant needed to work hard and go far afield, if he was to get any profit from his enterprises.

Nevertheless, these Jews owned horses and caravans, and sailed their own ships long before the time when great merchants, like the English Jew Antonio Fernandes Carvajal, traded in their own vessels between London and the Canaries. We hear of Palestinian Jews in the third century and of Italian Jews in the fifth century with ships of their own. Jewish sailors abounded on the Mediterranean, which tended to become a Jewish lake. The trade routes of the Jews were chiefly two. "By one route," says

Beazley, "they sailed from the ports of France and Italy to the Isthmus of Suez, and thence down the Red Sea to India and Farther Asia. By another course, they transported the goods of the West to the Syrian coast; up the Orontes to Antioch; down the Euphrates to Bassora; and so along the Persian Gulf to Oman and the Southern Ocean." Further, there were two chief overland routes. On the one side merchants left Spain, traversed the straits of Gibraltar, went by caravan from Tangier along the northern fringe of the desert, to Egypt, Syria, and Persia. This was the southern route. Then there was the northern route, through Germany, across the country of the Slavs to the Lower Volga; thence, descending the river, they sailed across the Caspian. Then the traveller proceeded along the Oxus valley to Balkh, and, turning north-east, traversed the country of the Tagazgaz Turks, and found himself at last on the frontier of China. When one realizes the extent of such a journey, it is not surprising to hear that the greatest authorities are agreed that in the Middle Ages, before the rise of the Italian trading republics, the Jews were the chief middlemen between Europe and Asia. Their vast commercial undertakings were productive of much good. Not only did the Jews bring to Europe new articles of food and luxury, but they served the various States as envoys and as intelligencers. The great Anglo-Jewish merchant Carvajal provided Cromwell with valuable information, as other Jewish merchants had done to other rulers of whom they were loyal servants. In the fifteenth century Henry of Portugal applied to Jews for intelligence respecting the interior of Africa, and a little later John, king of the same land, derived accurate information respecting India from two Jewish travellers that had spent many years at Ormuz and Calcutta. But it is unnecessary to add more facts of this type. The Jewish merchant traveller was no mere tradesman. He observed the country, especially did he note the numbers and occupations of the Jews, their synagogues, their schools, their vices, and their virtues.

  In truth, the Jewish traveller, as he got farther from home, was more at home than many of his contemporaries of other faiths when they were at home. He kept alive that sense of the oneness of Judaism which could be most strongly and completely achieved because there was no political bias to separate it into hostile camps.

But the interest between the traveller and his home was maintained by another bond. A striking feature of Jewish wayfaring life was the writing of letters home. The "Book of the Pious," composed about 1200, says: "He that departs from the city where his father and mother live, and travels to a place of danger, and his father and mother are anxious on account of him; it is the bounden duty of the son to hire a messenger as soon as he can and despatch a letter to his father and mother, telling them when he departs from the place of danger, that their anxiety may be allayed." Twice a year all Jews wrote family letters, at the New Year and the Passover, and they sent special greetings on birthdays. But the traveller was the chief letter-writer. "O my father," wrote the famous Obadiah of Bertinoro, in 1488, "my departure from thee has caused thee sorrow and suffering, and I am inconsolable that I was forced to leave at the time when age was creeping on thee. When I think of thy grey hairs, which I no longer see, my eyes flow over with tears. But if the happiness of serving thee in person is denied to me, yet I can at least serve thee as thou desirest, by writing to thee of my journey, by pouring my soul out to thee, by a full narrative of what I have seen and of the state and manners of the Jews in all the places where I have dwelt." After a long and valuable narrative, he concludes in this loving strain: "I have taken me a house in Jerusalem near the synagogue, and my window overlooks it. In the court where my house is, there live five women, and only one other man besides myself. He is blind, and his wife attends to my needs. God be thanked, I have escaped the sickness which affects nearly all travellers here. And I entreat you, weep not at my absence, but rejoice in my joy, that I am in the Holy City. I take God to witness that here the thought of all my sufferings vanishes, and but one image is before my eyes, thy dear face, O my father. Let me feel that I can picture that face to me, not clouded with tears, but lit with joy. You have other children around you; make them your joy, and let my letters, which I will ever and anon renew, bring solace to your age, as your letters bring solace to me."

Much more numerous than the epistles of sons to fathers are the letters of fathers to their families. When these come from Palestine, there is the same mingling of pious joy and human sorrow–joy to be in the Holy Land, sorrow to be separated from home. Another source of grief was the desolation of Palestine.

One such letter-writer tells sadly how he walked through the market at Zion, thought of the past, and only kept back his tears lest the Arab onlookers should see and ridicule his sorrow. Yet another medieval letter-writer, Nachmanides, reaches the summit of sentiment in these lines, which I take from Dr. Schechter's translation: "I was exiled by force from home, I left my sons and daughters; and with the dear and sweet ones whom I brought up on my knees, I left my soul behind me. My heart and my eyes will dwell with them forever. But O! the joy of a day in thy courts, O Jerusalem! visiting the ruins of the Temple and crying over the desolate Sanctuary; where I am permitted to caress thy stones, to fondle thy dust, and to weep over thy ruins. I wept bitterly, but found joy in my tears."

And with this thought in our mind we will take leave of our subject. It is the traveller who can best discern, amid the ruins wrought by man, the hope of a Divine rebuilding. Over the heavy hills of strife, he sees the coming dawn of peace. The world must still pass through much tribulation before the new Jerusalem shall arise, to enfold in its loving embrace all countries and all men. But the traveller, more than any other, hastens the good time. He overbridges seas, he draws nations nearer; he shows men that there are many ways of living and of loving. He teaches them to be tolerant; he humanizes them by presenting their brothers to them. The traveller it is who prepares a way in the wilderness, who makes straight in the desert a highway for the Lord.

The Fox's Heart

Pliny says that by eating the palpitating heart of a mole one acquires the faculty of divining future events. In "Westward Ho!" the Spanish prisoners beseech their English foe, Mr. Oxenham, not to leave them in the hands of the Cimaroons, for the latter invariably ate the hearts of all that fell into their hands, after roasting them alive. "Do you know," asks Mr. Alston in the "Witch's Head," "what those Basutu devils would have done if they had caught us? They would have skinned us, and made our hearts into mouti [medicine] and eaten them, to give them the courage of the white man." Ibn Verga, the author of a sixteenth century account of Jewish martyrs, records the following strange story: "I have heard that some people in Spain once brought the accusation that they had found, in the house of a Jew, a lad slain, and his breast rent near the heart. They asserted that the Jews had extracted his heart to employ it at their festival. Don Solomon, the Levite, who was a learned man and a Cabbalist, placed the Holy Name under the lad's tongue. The lad then awoke and told who had slain him, and who had removed his heart, with the object of accusing the poor Jews. I have not," adds the author of the Shebet Jehudah, "seen this story in writing, but I have heard it related."

We have the authority of Dr. Ploss for the statement that among the Slavs witches produce considerable disquiet in families, into which, folk say, they penetrate in the disguise of hens or butterflies. They steal the hearts of children in order to eat them. They strike the child on the left side with a little rod; the breast opens, and the witches tear out the heart, and devour every atom of it. Thereupon the wound closes up of itself, without leaving a trace of what has been done. The child dies either immediately or soon afterwards, as the witch chooses. Many children's illnesses are attributed to this cause. If one of these witches is caught asleep, the people seize her, and move her so as to place her head where her feet were before. On awaking, she has lost all her power for evil, and is transformed into a medicine-woman, who is acquainted with the healing effects of every herb, and aids in curing children of their diseases. In Heine's poem, "The Pilgrimage to Kevlaar," the love-lorn youth seeks the cure of his heart's ill by placing a waxen heart on the shrine. This is unquestionably the most exquisite use in literature of the heart as a charm.

Two or three of the stories that I have noted down on the gruesome subject of heart-eating have been given above. Such ideas were abhorrent to the Jewish conscience, and the use of the heart torn from a living animal was regarded as characteristic of idolatry (Jerusalem Talmud, Aboda Zara, ii, 41b). In the Book of Tobit a fish's heart plays a part, but it is detached from the dead animal, and is not eaten. It forms an ingredient of the smoke which exorcises the demon that is troubling the heroine Sarah.

I have not come across any passage in the Jewish Midrashim that ascribes to "heart-eating," even in folk-lore, the virtue of bestowing wisdom. Aristotle seems to lend his authority to some such notion as that I have quoted from Pliny, when he says, "Man alone presents the phenomenon of heart-beating, because he alone is moved by hope and by expectation of what is coming." As George H. Lewes remarked, it is quite evident that Aristotle could never have held a bird in his hand. The idea, however, that eating the heart of an animal has wisdom-conferring virtue seems to underlie a very interesting Hebrew fable published by Dr. Steinschneider, in his Alphabetum Siracidis. The Angel of Death had demanded of God the power to slay all living things.

"The Holy One replied, 'Cast a pair of each species into the sea, and then thou shalt have dominion over all that remain of the species.' The Angel did so forthwith, and he cast a pair of each kind into the sea. When the fox saw what he was about, what did he do? At once he stood and wept. Then said the Angel of Death unto him, 'Why weepest thou?' 'For my companions, whom thou hast cast into the sea,' answered the fox. 'Where, then, are thy companions?' said the Angel. The fox ran to the sea-shore [with his wife], and the Angel of Death beheld the reflection of the fox in the water, and he thought that he had already cast in a pair of foxes, so, addressing the fox by his side, he cried, 'Be off with you!' The fox at once fled and escaped. The weasel met him, and the fox related what had happened, and what he had done; and so the weasel went and did likewise.

"At the end of the year, the leviathan assembled all the creatures in the sea, and lo! the fox and the weasel were missing, for they had not come into the sea. He sent to ask, and he was told how the fox and the weasel had escaped through their wisdom. They taunted the leviathan, saying, 'The fox is exceedingly cunning.' The leviathan felt uneasy and envious, and he sent a deputation of great fishes, with the order that they were to deceive the fox, and bring him before him. They went, and found him by the sea-shore. When the fox saw the fishes disporting themselves near the bank, he was surprised, and he went among them. They beheld him, and asked, 'Who art thou?' 'I am the fox,' said he. 'Knowest thou not,' continued the fishes, 'that a great honor is in store for thee, and that we have come here on thy behalf?' 'What is it?' asked the fox. 'The leviathan,' they said, 'is sick, and like to die. He has appointed thee to reign in his stead, for he has heard that thou art wiser and more prudent than all other animals. Come with us, for we are his messengers, and are here to thy honor.' 'But,' objected the fox, 'how can I come into the sea without being drowned?' 'Nay,' said the fishes; 'ride upon one of us, and he will carry thee above the sea, so that not even a drop of water shall touch so much as the soles of thy feet, until thou reachest the kingdom. We will take thee down without thy knowing it. Come with us, and reign over us, and be king, and be joyful all thy days. No more wilt thou need to seek for food, nor will wild beasts, stronger than thou, meet thee and devour thee.'

"The fox heard and believed their words. He rode upon one of them, and they went with him into the sea. Soon, however, the waves dashed over him, and he began to perceive that he had been tricked. 'Woe is me!' wailed the fox, 'what have I done? I have played many a trick on others, but these fishes have played one on me worth all mine put together. Now I have fallen into their hands, how shall I free myself? Indeed,' he said, turning to the fishes, 'now that I am fully in your power, I shall speak the truth. What are you going to do with me?' 'To tell thee the truth,' replied the fishes, 'the leviathan has heard thy fame, that thou art very wise, and he said, I will rend the fox, and will eat his heart, and thus I shall become wise.' 'Oh!' said the fox, 'why did you not tell me the truth at first? I should then have brought my heart with me, and I should have given it to King Leviathan, and he would have honored me; but now ye are in an evil plight.' 'What! thou hast not thy heart with thee?' 'Certainly not. It is our custom to leave our heart at home while we go about from place to place. When we need our heart, we take it; otherwise it remains at home.' 'What must we do?' asked the bewildered fishes. 'My house and dwelling-place,' replied the fox, 'are by the sea-shore. If you like, carry me back to the place whence you brought me, I will fetch my heart, and will come again with you. I will present my heart to Leviathan, and he will reward me and you with honors. But if you take me thus, without my heart, he will be wroth with you, and will devour you. I have no fear for myself, for I shall say unto him: My lord, they did not tell me at first, and when they did tell me, I begged them to return for my heart, but they refused.' The fishes at once declared that he was speaking well. They conveyed him back to the spot on the sea-shore whence they had taken him. Off jumped the fox, and he danced with joy. He threw himself on the sand, and laughed. 'Be quick,' cried the fishes, 'get thy heart, and come.' But the fox answered, 'You fools! Begone! How could I have come with you without my heart? Have you any animals that go about without their hearts?' 'Thou hast tricked us,' they moaned. 'Fools! I tricked the Angel of Death, how much more easily a parcel of silly fishes.'

"They returned in shame, and related to their master what had happened. 'In truth,' he said, 'he is cunning, and ye are simple. Concerning you was it said, The turning away of the simple shall slay them [Prov. i:32]. Then the leviathan ate the fishes."

Metaphorically, the Bible characterizes the fool as a man "without a heart," and it is probably in the same sense that modern Arabs describe the brute creation as devoid of hearts. The fox in the narrative just given knew better. Not so, however, the lady who brought a curious question for her Rabbi to solve. The case to which I refer may be found in the Responsa Zebi Hirsch. Hirsch's credulous questioner asserted that she had purchased a live cock, but on killing and drawing it, she had found that it possessed no heart. The Rabbi refused very properly to believe her. On investigating the matter, he found that, while she was dressing the cock, two cats had been standing near the table. The Rabbi assured his questioner that there was no need to inquire further into the whereabouts of the cock's heart.

Out of the crowd of parallels to the story of the fox's heart supplied by the labors of Benfey, I select one given in the second volume of the learned investigator's Pantschatantra. A crocodile had formed a close friendship with a monkey, who inhabited a tree close to the water side. The monkey gave the crocodile nuts, which the latter relished heartily. One day the crocodile took some of the nuts home to his wife. She found them excellent, and inquired who was the donor. "If," she said, when her husband had told her, "he feeds on such ambrosial nuts, this monkey's heart must be ambrosia itself. Bring me his heart, that I may eat it, and so be free from age and death." Does not this version supply a more probable motive than that attributed in the Hebrew story to the leviathan? I strongly suspect that the Hebrew fable has been pieced together from various sources, and that the account given by the fishes, viz. that the leviathan was ill, was actually the truth in the original story. The leviathan would need the fox's heart, not to become wise, but in order to save his life.

To return to the crocodile. He refuses to betray his friend, and his wife accuses him of infidelity. His friend, she maintains, is not a monkey at all, but a lady-love of her husband's. Else why should he hesitate to obey her wishes? "If he is not your beloved, why will you not kill him? Unless you bring me his heart, I will not taste food, but will die." Then the crocodile gives in, and in the most friendly manner invites the monkey to pay him and his wife a visit. The monkey consents unsuspectingly, but discovers the truth, and escapes by adopting the same ruse as that employed by the fox. He asserts that he has left his heart behind on his tree.

That eating the heart of animals was not thought a means of obtaining wisdom among the Jews, may be directly inferred from a passage in the Talmud (Horayoth, 13b). Among five things there enumerated as "causing a man to forget what he has learned," the Talmud includes "eating the hearts of animals." Besides, in certain well-known stories in the Midrash, where a fox eats some other animal's heart, his object is merely to enjoy a titbit.

One such story in particular deserves attention. There are at least three versions of it. The one is contained in the Mishle Shualim, or "Fox-Stories," by Berechiah ha-Nakdan (no. 106), the second in the Hadar Zekenim (fol. 27b), and the third in the Midrash Yalkut, on Exodus (ed. Venice, 56a). Let us take the three versions in the order named.

A wild boar roams in a lion's garden. The lion orders him to quit the place and not defile his residence. The boar promises to obey, but next morning he is found near the forbidden precincts. The lion orders one of his ears to be cut off. He then summons the fox, and directs that if the boar still persists in his obnoxious visits, no mercy shall be shown to him. The boar remains obstinate, and loses his ears (one had already gone!) and eyes, and finally he is killed. The lion bids the fox prepare the carcass for His Majesty's repast, but the fox himself devours the boar's heart. When the lion discovers the loss, the fox quiets his master by asking, "If the boar had possessed a heart, would he have been so foolish as to disobey you so persistently?"

The king of the beasts, runs the story in the second of the three versions, appointed the ass as keeper of the tolls. One day King Lion, together with the wolf and the fox, approached the city. The ass came and demanded the toll of them. Said the fox, "You are the most audacious of animals. Don't you see that the king is with us?" But the ass answered, "The king himself shall pay," and he went and demanded the toll of the king. The lion rent him to pieces, and the fox ate the heart, and excused himself as in the former version.

The Yalkut, or third version, is clearly identical with the preceding, for, like it, the story is quoted to illustrate the Scriptural text referring to Pharaoh's heart becoming hard. In this version, however, other animals accompany the lion and the fox, and the scene of the story is on board ship. The ass demands the fare, with the same dénouement as before.

What induced the fox to eat the victim's heart? The ass is not remarkable for wisdom, nor is the boar. Hence the wily Reynard can scarcely have thought to add to his store of cunning by his surreptitious meal.

Hearts, in folk-lore, have been eaten for revenge, as in the grim story of the lover's heart told by Boccaccio. The jealous husband forces his wife, whose fidelity he doubts, to make a meal of her supposed lover's heart. In the story of the great bird's egg, again, the brother who eats the heart becomes rich, but not wise. Various motives, no doubt, are assigned in other Märchen for choosing the heart; but in these particular Hebrew fables, it is merely regarded as a bonne bouche. Possibly the Talmudic caution, that eating the heart of a beast brings forgetfulness, may have a moral significance; it may mean that one who admits bestial passions into his soul will be destitute of a mind for nobler thoughts. This suggestion I have heard, and I give it for what it may be worth. As a rule, there is no morality in folk-lore; stories with morals belong to the later and more artificial stage of poet-lore. Homiletical folk-lore, of course, stands on a different basis.

Now, in the Yalkut version of the fox and the lion fable, all that we are told is, "The fox saw the ass's heart; he took it, and ate it." But Berechiah leaves us in no doubt as to the fox's motive. "The fox saw that his heart was fat, and so he took it." In the remaining version, "The fox saw that the heart was good, so he ate it." This needs no further comment.

Of course, it has been far from my intention to dispute that the heart was regarded by Jews as the seat both of the intellect and the feelings, of all mental and spiritual functions, indeed. The heart was the best part of man, the fount of life; hence Jehudah Halevi's well-known saying, "Israel is to the world as the heart to the body." An intimate connection was also established, by Jews and Greeks alike, between the physical condition of the heart and man's moral character. It was a not unnatural thought that former ages were more pious than later times. "The heart of Rabbi Akiba was like the door of the porch [which was twenty cubits high], the heart of Rabbi Eleazar ben Shammua was like the door of the Temple [this was only ten cubits high], while our hearts are only as large as the eye of a needle." But I am going beyond my subject. To collect all the things, pretty and the reverse, that have been said in Jewish literature about the heart, would need more leisure, and a great deal more learning, than I possess. So I will conclude with a story, pathetic as well as poetical, from a Jewish medieval chronicle.

A Mohammedan king once asked a learned Rabbi why the Jews, who had in times long past been so renowned for their bravery, had in later generations become subdued, and even timorous. The Rabbi, to prove that captivity and persecution were the cause of the change, proposed an experiment. He bade the king take two lion's whelps, equally strong and big. One was tied up, the other was allowed to roam free in the palace grounds. They were fed alike, and after an interval both were killed. The king's officers found that the heart of the captive lion was but one-tenth as large as that of his free companion, thus evidencing the degenerating influence of slavery. This is meant, no doubt, as a fable, but, at least, it is not without a moral. The days of captivity are gone, and it may be hoped that Jewish large-heartedness has come back with the breath of freedom.

"Marriages Are Made in Heaven"

"The Omnipresent," said a Rabbi, "is occupied in making marriages." The levity of the saying lies in the ear of him who hears it; for by marriages the speaker meant all the wondrous combinations of the universe, whose issue makes our good and evil."

-- George Eliot

The proverb that I have set at the head of these lines is popular in every language of Europe. Need I add that a variant may be found in Chinese? The Old Man of the Moon unites male and female with a silken, invisible thread, and they cannot afterwards be separated, but are destined to become man and wife. The remark of the Rabbi quoted in "Daniel Deronda" carries the proverb back apparently to a Jewish origin; and it is, indeed, more than probable that the Rabbinical literature is the earliest source to which this piece of folk-philosophy can be traced.

George Eliot's Rabbi was Jose bar Chalafta, and his remark was made to a lady, possibly a Roman matron of high quality, in Sepphoris. Rabbi Jose was evidently an adept in meeting the puzzling questions of women, for as many as sixteen interviews between him and "matrons" are recorded in Agadic literature. Whether because prophetic of its subsequent popularity, or for some other reason, this particular dialogue in which Rabbi Jose bore so conspicuous a part is repeated in the Midrash Rabba alone not less than four times, besides appearing in other Midrashim. It will be as well, then, to reproduce the passage in a summarized form, for it may be fairly described as the locus classicus on the subject.

"How long," she asked, "did it take God to create the world?" and Rabbi Jose informed her that the time occupied was six days. "What has God been doing since that time?" continued the matron. "The Holy One," answered the Rabbi, "has been sitting in Heaven arranging marriages."–"Indeed!" she replied, "I could do as much myself. I have thousands of slaves, and could marry them off in couples in a single hour. It is easy enough."–"I hope that you will find it so," said Rabbi Jose. "In Heaven it is thought as difficult as the dividing of the Red Sea." He then took his departure, while she assembled one thousand men-servants and as many maid-servants, and, marking them off in pairs, ordered them all to marry. On the day following this wholesale wedding, the poor victims came to their mistress in a woeful plight. One had a broken leg, another a black eye, a third a swollen nose; all were suffering from some ailment, but with one voice they joined in the cry, "Lady, unmarry us again!" Then the matron sent for Rabbi Jose, admitted that she had underrated the delicacy and difficulty of match-making, and wisely resolved to leave Heaven for the future to do its work in its own way.

The moral conveyed by this story may seem, however, to have been idealized by George Eliot almost out of recognition. This is hardly the case. Genius penetrates into the heart, even from a casual glance at the face of things. Though it is unlikely that she had ever seen the full passages in the Midrash to which she was alluding, yet her insight was not at fault. For the saying that God is occupied in making marriages is, in fact, associated in some passages of the Midrash with the far wider problems of man's destiny, with the universal effort to explain the inequalities of fortune, and the changes with which the future is heavy.

Rabbi Jose's proverbial explanation of connubial happiness was not merely a bon mot invented on the spur of the moment, to silence an awkward questioner. It was a firm conviction, which finds expression in more than one quaint utterance, but also in more than one matter-of-fact assertion. To take the latter first:

"Rabbi Phineas in the name of Rabbi Abbahu said, We find in the Torah, in the Prophets, and in the Holy Writings, evidence that a man's wife is chosen for him by the Holy One, blessed be He. Whence do we deduce it in the Torah? From Genesis xxiv. 50: Then Laban and Bethuel answered and said [in reference to Rebekah's betrothal to Isaac], The thing proceedeth from the Lord. In the Prophets it is found in Judges xiv. 4 [where it is related how Samson wished to mate himself with a woman in Timnath, of the daughters of the Philistines], But his father and mother knew not that it was of the Lord. In the Holy Writings the same may be seen, for it is written (Proverbs xix. 14), House and riches are the inheritance of fathers, but a prudent wife is from the Lord."

Many years ago, a discussion was carried on in the columns of Notes and Queries concerning the origin of the saying round which my present desultory jottings are centred. One correspondent, with unconscious plagiarism, suggested that the maxim was derived from Proverbs xix. 14.

Another text that might be appealed to is Tobit vi. 18. The Angel encourages Tobit to marry Sarah, though her seven husbands, one after the other, had died on their wedding eves. "Fear not," said Raphael, "for she is appointed unto thee from the beginning."

Here we may, for a moment, pause to consider whether any parallels to the belief in Heaven-made marriages exist in other ancient literatures. It appears in English as early as Shakespeare:

God, the best maker of all marriages,
Combine your hearts in one.
>--Henry V., v. 2.

This, however, is too late to throw any light on its origin. With a little ingenuity, one might, perhaps, torture some such notion out of certain fantastic sentences of Plato. In the Symposium (par. 192), however, God is represented as putting obstacles in the way of the union of fitting lovers, in consequence of the wickedness of mankind. When men become, by their conduct, reconciled with God, they may find their true loves. Astrological divinations on the subject are certainly common enough in Eastern stories; a remarkable instance will be given later on. At the present day, Lane tells us, the numerical value of the letters in the names of the two parties to the contract are added for each name separately, and one of the totals is subtracted from the other. If the remainder is uneven, the inference drawn is favorable; but if even, the reverse. The pursuit of Gematria is apparently not limited to Jews. Such methods, however, hardly illustrate my present point, for the identity of the couple is not discovered by the process. Whether the diviner's object is to make this discovery, or the future lot of the married pair is all that he seeks to reveal, in both cases, though he charm never so wisely, it does not fall within the scope of this inquiry. Without stretching one's imagination too much, some passages in the Pantschatantra seem to imply a belief that marriage-making is under the direct control of Providence. Take, for instance, the story of the beautiful princess who was betrothed to a serpent, Deva Serma's son. Despite the various attempts made to induce her to break off so hideous a match, she declines steadfastly to go back from her word, and bases her refusal on the ground that the marriage was inevitable and destined by the gods.

    As quaint illustrations may be instanced the following: "Raba heard a certain man praying that he might marry a certain damsel; Raba rebuked him with the words: 'If she be destined for thee, nothing will part thee from her; if thou art not destined for her, thou art denying Providence in praying for her.' Afterwards Raba heard him say, 'If I am not destined to marry her, I hope that either I or she may die,'" meaning that he could not bear to witness her union with another. Despite Raba's protest, other instances are on record of prayers similar to the one of which he disapproved. Or, again, the Midrash offers a curious illustration of Psalm lxii. 10, "Surely men of low degree are a breath, and men of high degree a lie." The first clause of the verse alludes to those who say in the usual way of the world, that a certain man is about to wed a certain maiden, and the second clause to those who say that a certain maiden is about to wed a certain man. In both cases people are in error in thinking that the various parties are acting entirely of their own free will; as a matter of fact, the whole affair is predestined. I am not quite certain whether the same idea is intended by the Yalkut Reubeni, in which the following occurs: "Know that all religious and pious men in this our generation are henpecked by their wives, the reason being connected with the mystery of the Golden Calf. The men on that occasion did not protest against the action of the mixed multitude [at whose door the charge of making the calf is laid], while the women were unwilling to surrender their golden ornaments for idolatrous purposes. Therefore they rule over their husbands." One might also quote the bearing of the mystical theory of transmigration on the predestination of bridal pairs. In the Talmud, on the other hand, the virtues of a man's wife are sometimes said to be in proportion to the husband's own; or in other words, his own righteousness is the cause of his acquiring a good wife. The obvious objection, raised by the Talmud itself, is that a man's merits can hardly be displayed before his birth–and yet his bride is destined for him at that early period.

Yet more quaint (I should perhaps rather term it consistent, were not consistency rare enough to be indistinguishable from quaintness) was the confident belief of a maiden of whom mention is made in the Sefer ha-Chasidim (par. 384). She refused persistently to deck her person with ornaments. People said to her, "If you go about thus unadorned, no one will notice you nor court you." She replied with firm simplicity, "It is the Holy One, blessed be He, that settles marriages; I need have no concern on the point myself." Virtue was duly rewarded, for she married a learned and pious husband. This passage in the "Book of the Pious" reminds me of the circumstance under which the originator of the latter-day Chasidism, Israel Baalshem, is said to have married. When he was offered the daughter of a rich and learned man of Brody, named Abraham, he readily accepted the alliance, because he knew that Abraham's daughter was his bride destined by heaven. For, like Moses Mendelssohn, in some other respects the antagonist of the Chasidim, Baalshem accepted the declaration of Rabbi Judah in the name of Rab: "Forty days before the creation of a girl, a proclamation [Bath-Kol] is made in Heaven, saying, 'The daughter of such a one shall marry such and such a one.'"

The belief in the Divine ordaining of marriages affected the medieval Synagogue liturgy. To repeat what I have written elsewhere: When the bridegroom, with a joyous retinue, visited the synagogue on the Sabbath following his marriage, the congregation chanted the chapter of Genesis (xxiv) that narrates the story of Isaac's marriage, which, as Abraham's servant claimed, was providentially arranged. This chapter was sung, not only in Hebrew, but in Arabic, in countries where the latter language was the vernacular. These special readings, which were additional to the regular Scripture lesson, seem to have fallen out of use in Europe in the seventeenth century, but they are still retained in the East. But all over Jewry the beautiful old belief is contained in the wording of the fourth of the "seven benedictions" sung at the celebration of a wedding, "Blessed art thou, O Lord our God, King of the Universe, who hast made man in thine image, after thy likeness, and hast prepared unto him out of his very self a perpetual fabric." Here is recalled the creation of Eve, of whom God Himself said, "I will make for man a help meet unto him." Not only the marriage, but also the bride was Heaven-made, and the wonderful wedding benediction enshrines this idea.

In an Agadic story, the force of this predestination is shown to be too strong even for royal opposition. It does not follow that the pre-arrangement of marriages implies that the pair cannot fall in love of their own accord. On the contrary, just the right two eventually come together; for once freewill and destiny need present no incompatibility. The combination, here shadowed, of a predestined and yet true-love marriage, is effectively illustrated in what follows:

"Solomon the king was blessed with a very beautiful daughter; she was the fairest maiden in the whole land of Israel. Her father observed the stars, to discover by astrology who was destined to be her mate in life and wed her, when lo! he saw that his future son-in-law would be the poorest man in the nation. Now, what did Solomon do? He built a high tower by the sea, and surrounded it on all sides with inaccessible walls; he then took his daughter and placed her in the tower under the charge of seventy aged guardians. He supplied the castle with provisions, but he had no door made in it, so that none could enter the fortress without the knowledge of the guard. Then the king said, 'I will watch in what way God will work the matter.'

"In course of time, a poor and weary traveller was walking on his way by night, his garments were ragged and torn, he was barefooted and ready to faint with hunger, cold, and fatigue. He knew not where to sleep, but, casting his eyes around him, he beheld the skeleton of an ox lying on a field hard by. The youth crept inside the skeleton to shelter himself from the wind, and, while he slept there, down swooped a great bird, which lifted up the carcass and the unconscious youth in it. The bird flew with its burden to the top of Solomon's tower, and set it down on the roof before the very door of the imprisoned princess. She went forth on the morrow to walk on the roof according to her daily wont, and she descried the youth. She said to him, 'Who art thou? and who brought thee hither?' He answered, 'I am a Jew of Acco, and a bird bore me to thee.' The kind-hearted maiden clothed him in new garments; they bathed and anointed him, and she saw that he was the handsomest youth in Israel. They loved one another, and his soul was bound up in hers. One day she said, 'Wilt thou marry me?' He replied, 'Would it might be so!' They resolved to marry. But there was no ink with which to write the Kethubah, or marriage certificate. Love laughs at obstacles. So, using some drops of his own blood as ink, the marriage was secretly solemnized, and he said, 'God is my witness to-day, and Michael and Gabriel likewise.' When the matter leaked out, the dismayed custodians of the princess hastily summoned Solomon. The king at once obeyed their call, and asked for the presumptuous youth. He looked at his son-in-law, inquired of him as to his father and mother, family and dwelling-place, and from his replies the king recognized him for the selfsame man whom he had seen in the stars as the destined husband of his daughter. Then Solomon rejoiced with exceeding joy and exclaimed, Blessed is the Omnipresent who giveth a wife to man and establisheth him in his house."

The moral of which seems to be that, though marriages are made in Heaven, love must be made on earth.

Hebrew Love Songs

Palestine is still the land of song. There the peasant sings Arabic ditties in the field when he sows and reaps, in the desert when he tends his flock, at the oasis when the caravan rests for the night, and when camels are remounted next morning. The maiden's fresh voice keeps droning rhythm with her hands and feet as she carries water from the well or wood from the scanty forest, when she milks the goats, and when she bakes the bread.

The burden of a large portion of these songs is love. The love motive is most prominent musically during the long week of wedding festivities, but it is by no means limited to these occasions. The songs often contain an element of quaint, even arch, repartee, in which the girl usually has the better of the argument. Certainly the songs are sometimes gross, but only in the sense that they are vividly natural. With no delicacy of expression, they are seldom intrinsically coarse. The troubadours of Europe trilled more daintily of love, but there was at times an illicit note in their lays. Eastern love songs never attain the ideal purity of Dante, but they hardly ever sink to the level of Ovid.

But why begin an account of Hebrew love songs by citing extant Palestinian examples in Arabic? Because there is an undeniable, if remote, relationship between some of the latter and the Biblical Song of Songs. In that marvellous poem, outspoken praise of earthly beauty, frank enumeration of the physical charms of the lovers, thorough unreserve of imagery, are conspicuous enough. Just these features, as Wetzstein showed, are reproduced, in a debased, yet recognizable, likeness, by the modern Syrian wasf–a lyric description of the bodily perfections and adornments of a newly-wed pair. The Song of Songs, or Canticles, it is true, is hardly a marriage ode or drama; its theme is betrothed faith rather than marital affection. Still, if we choose to regard the Song of Songs as poetry merely of the wasf type, the Hebrew is not only far older than any extant Arabic instance, but it transcends the wasf type as a work of inspired genius transcends conventional exercises in verse-making. There are superficial similarities between the wasf and Canticles, but there is no spiritual kinship. The wasf is to the Song as Lovelace is to Shakespeare, nay, the distance is even greater. The difference is not only of degree, it is essential. The one touches the surface of love, the other sounds its depths. The Song of Songs immeasurably surpasses the wasf even as poetry. It has been well said by Dr. Harper (author of the best English edition of Canticles), that, viewed simply as poetry, the Song of Songs belongs to the loveliest masterpieces of art. "If, as Milton said, 'poetry should be simple, sensuous, passionate,' then here we have poetry of singular beauty and power. Such unaffected delight in all things fair as we find here is rare in any literature, and is especially remarkable in ancient Hebrew literature. The beauty of the world and of the creatures in it has been so deeply and warmly felt, that even to-day the ancient poet's emotion of joy in them thrills through the reader."

It is superfluous to justify this eulogy by quotation. It is impossible also, unless the quotation extend to the whole book. Yet one scene shall be cited, the exquisite, lyrical dialogue of spring, beginning with the tenth verse of the second chapter. It is a dialogue, though the whole is reported by one speaker, the Shulammite maid. Her shepherd lover calls to her as she stands hidden behind a lattice, in the palace in Lebanon, whither she has been decoyed, or persuaded to go, by the "ladies of Jerusalem."

The shepherd lover calls
  Rise up, my love,
    My fair one, come away!
  For, lo, the winter is past,
  The rain is over and gone,
  The flowers appear on the earth:
  The birds' singing time is here,
  And the voice of the turtle-dove is heard in our land.
  The fig-tree ripens red her winter fruit,
  And blossoming vines give forth fragrance.
  Rise up, my love,
    My fair one, come away!

Shulammith makes no answer, though she feels that the shepherd is conscious of her presence. She is, as it were, in an unapproachable steep, such as the wild dove selects for her shy nest. So he goes on:

    O my dove, that art in the clefts of the rock,
      In the covert of the steep!
    Let me see thy face,

> Let me hear thy voice,
> For sweet is thy voice, and thy face comely!

She remains tantalizingly invisible, but becomes audible. She sings a snatch from a vineyard-watcher's song, hinting, perhaps, at the need in which her person (her "vineyard" as she elsewhere calls it) stands of protection against royal foxes, small and large.

Shulammith sings
  Take us the foxes,
  The little foxes,
    That spoil the vineyards:
  For our vines are in blossom!
Then, in loving rapture,

Shulammith speaks in an aside
  My beloved is mine, and I am his:
  He feedeth his flock among the lilies!

But she cannot refuse her lover one glance at herself, even though she appear only to warn him of his danger, to urge him to leave her and return when the day is over.

Shulammith entreatingly to her lover
  Until the evening breeze blows,
  And the shadows disappear (at sunset),
  Turn, my beloved!
  Be thou as a young hart
  Upon the cleft-riven hills!

This is but one of the many dainty love idylls of this divine poem. Or, again, "could the curious helplessness of the dreamer in a dream and the yearning of a maiden's affection be more exquisitely expressed than in the lines beginning, I was asleep, but my heart waked"? But, indeed, as the critic I am quoting continues, "the felicities of expression and the happy imaginings of the poem are endless. The spring of nature and of love has been caught and fixed in its many exquisite lines, as only Shakespeare elsewhere has done it; and, understood as we think it must be understood, it has that ethical background of sacrifice and self-forgetting which all love must have to be thoroughly worthy."

It is this ethical, or, as I prefer to term it, spiritual, background that discriminates the Song of Songs on the one hand from the Idylls of Theocritus, and, on the other, from the Syrian popular ditties. Some moderns, notably Budde, hold that the Book of Canticles is merely a collection of popular songs used at Syrian weddings, in which the bride figures as queen and her mate as king, just as Budde (wrongly) conceives them to figure in the Biblical Song. Budde suggests that there were "guilds of professional singers at weddings, and that we have in the Song of Songs simply the repertoire of some ancient guild-brother, who, in order to assist his memory, wrote down at random all the songs he could remember, or those he thought the best."

But this theory has been generally rejected as unsatisfying. The book, despite its obscurities, is clearly a unity. It is no haphazard collection of love songs. There is a sustained dramatic action leading up to a noble climax. Some passages almost defy the attempt to fit them into a coherent plot, but most moderns detect the following story in Canticles: A beautiful maid of Shulem (perhaps another form of Shunem), beloved by a shepherd swain, is the only daughter of well-off but rustic parents. She is treated harshly by her brothers, who set her to watch the vineyards, and this exposure to the sun somewhat mars her beauty. Straying in the gardens, she is on a day in spring surprised by Solomon and his train, who are on a royal progress to the north. She is taken to the palace in the capital, and later to a royal abode in Lebanon. There the "ladies of Jerusalem" seek to win her affections for the king, who himself pays her his court. But she resists all blandishments, and remains faithful to her country lover. Surrendering graciously to her strenuous resistance, Solomon permits her to return unharmed to her mountain home. Her lover meets her, and as she draws near her native village, the maid, leaning on the shepherd's arm, breaks forth into the glorious panegyric of love, which, even if it stood alone, would make the poem deathless. But it does not stand alone. It is in every sense a climax to what has gone before. And what a climax! It is a vindication of true love, which weighs no allurements of wealth and position against itself; a love of free inclination, yet altogether removed from license. Nor is it an expression of that lower love which may prevail in a polygamous state of society, when love is dissipated among many. We have here the love of one for one, an exclusive and absorbing devotion. For though the Bible never prohibited polygamy, the Jews had become monogamous from the Babylonian Exile at latest. The splendid praise of the virtuous woman at the end of the Book of Proverbs gives a picture, not only of monogamous home-life, but of woman's influence at its highest. The virtuous woman of Proverbs is wife and mother, deft guide of the home, open-handed dispenser of charity, with the law of kindness on her tongue; but her activity also extends to the world outside the home, to the mart, to the business of life. Where, in olden literature, are woman's activities wider or more manifold, her powers more fully developed? Now, the Song of Songs is the lyric companion to this prose picture. The whole Song works up towards the description of love in the last chapter–towards the culmination of the thought and feeling of the whole series of episodes. The Shulammite speaks:

> Set me as a seal upon thy heart,
> As a seal upon thine arm:
> For love is strong as death,
> Jealousy is cruel as the grave:
> The flashes thereof are flashes of fire,
> A very flame of God!
> Many waters cannot quench love,
> Neither can the floods drown it:
> If a man would give the substance of his house for love,
> He would be utterly contemned.

The vindication of the Hebrew song from degradation to the level of the Syrian wasf is easy enough. But some may feel that there is more plausibility in the case that has been set up for the connection between Canticles and another type of love song, the Idylls of Theocritus, the Sicilian poet whose Greek compositions gave lyric distinction to the Ptolemaic court at Alexandria, about the middle of the third century B.C.E. It is remarkable how reluctant some writers are to admit originality in ideas. Such writers seem to recognize no possibility other than supposing Theocritus to have copied Canticles, or Canticles Theocritus. It does not occur to them that both may be original, independent expressions of similar emotions. Least original among ideas is this denial of originality in ideas. Criticism has often stultified itself under the obsession that everything is borrowed. On this theory there can never have been an original note. The poet, we are told, is born, not made; but poetry, apparently, is always made, never born.

The truth rather is that as human nature is everywhere similar, there must necessarily be some similarity in its literary expression. This is emphatically the case with the expression given to the emotional side of human nature. The love of man for maid, rising everywhere from the same spring, must find lyric outlets that look a good deal alike. The family resemblance between the love poems of various peoples is due to the elemental kinship of the love. Every true lover is original, yet most true lovers, including those who have no familiarity with poetical literature, fall instinctively on the same terms of endearment. Differences only make themselves felt in the spiritual attitudes of various ages and races towards love. Theocritus has been compared to Canticles, by some on the ground of certain Orientalisms of his thought and phrases, as in his Praise of Ptolemy. But his love poems bear no trace of Orientalism in feeling, as Canticles shows no trace of Hellenism in its conception of love. The similarities are human, the differences racial.

Direct literary imitation of love lyrics certainly does occur. Virgil imitated Theocritus, and the freshness of the Greek Idyll became the convention of the Roman Eclogue. When such conscious imitation takes place, it is perfectly obvious. There is no mistaking the affectation of an urban lyrist, whose lovers masquerade as shepherds in the court of Louis XIV.

Theocritus seems to have had earlier Greek models, but few readers of his Idylls can question his originality, and fewer still will agree with Mahaffy in denying the naturalness of his goatherds and fishermen, in a word, his genuineness. Mahaffy wavers between two statements, that the Idylls are an affectation for Alexandria, and sincere for Sicily. The two statements are by no means contradictory. Much the same thing is true of Canticles, the Biblical Song of Songs. It is unreasonable for anyone who has seen or read about a Palestinian spring, with its unique beauty of flower and bird and blossom, to imagine that the author of Canticles needed or used second-hand sources of inspiration, however little his drama may have accorded with the life of Jerusalem in the Hellenistic period. And as the natural scenic background in each case is native, so is the treatment of the love theme; in both it is passionate, but in the one it is nothing else, in the other it is also spiritual. In both, the whole is artistic, but not artificial. As regards the originality of the love-interest in Canticles, it must suffice to say that there was always a strong romantic strain in the Jewish character.

Canticles is perhaps (by no means certainly) post-Exilic and not far removed in date from the age of Theocritus. Still, a post-Exilic Hebrew poet had no more reason to go abroad for a romantic plot than Hosea, or the author of Ruth, or the writer of the royal Epithalamium (Psalm xlv), an almost certainly pre-Exilic composition. This Psalm has been well termed a "prelude to the Song of Songs," for in a real sense Canticles is anticipated and even necessitated by it. In Ruth we have a romance of the golden corn-field, and the author chooses the unsophisticated days of the Judges as the setting of his tale. In Canticles we have a contrasted picture between the simplicity of shepherd-life and the urban voluptuousness which was soon to attain its climax in the court of the Ptolemies. So the poet chose the luxurious reign of Solomon as the background for his exquisite "melodrama." Both Ruth and Canticles are home-products, and ancient Greek literature has no real parallel to either.

Yet, despite the fact that the Hebrew Bible is permeated through and through, in its history, its psalmody, and its prophetic oratory, with images drawn from love, especially in rustic guise, so competent a critic as Graetz conceived that the pastoral background of the love-story of Canticles must have been artificial. While most of those who have accepted the theory of imitation-they cannot have reread the Idylls and the Song as wholes to persist in such a theory-have contended that Theocritus borrowed from Canticles, Graetz is convinced that the Hebrew poet must have known and imitated the Greek idyllist. The hero and heroine of the Song, he thinks, are not real shepherds; they are bucolic dilettanti, their shepherd-rôle is not serious. Whence, then, this superficial pastoral mise-en-scène? This critic, be it observed, places Canticles in the Ptolemaic age.

"In the then Judean world," writes Graetz, "in the post-Exilic period, pastoral life was in no way so distinguished as to serve as a poetic foil. On the contrary, the shepherd was held in contempt. Agriculture was so predominant that large herds were considered a detriment; they spoiled the grain. Shepherds, too, were esteemed robbers, in that they allowed their cattle to graze on the lands of others. In Judea itself, in the post-Exilic period, there were few pasture-grounds for such nomads. Hence the song transfers the goats to Gilead, where there still existed grazing-places. In the Judean world the poet could find nothing to suggest the idealization of the shepherd. As he, nevertheless, represents the simple life, as opposed to courtly extravagance, through the figures of shepherds, he must have worked from a foreign model. But Theocritus was the first perfect pastoral poet. Through his influence shepherd songs became a favorite genre. He had no lack of imitators. Theocritus had full reason to contrast court and rustic life and idealize the latter, for in his native Sicily there were still shepherds in primitive simplicity. Under his influence and that of his followers, it became the fashion to represent the simple life in pastoral guise. The poet of Canticles–who wrote for cultured circles–was forced to make use of the convention. But, as though to excuse himself for taking a Judean shepherd as a representative of the higher virtues, he made his shepherd one who feeds among the lilies. It is not the rude neat-herds of Gilead or the Judean desert that hold such noble dialogues, but shepherds of delicate refinement. In a word, the whole eclogic character of Canticles appears to be copied from the Theocritan model."

This contention would be conclusive, if it were based on demonstrable facts. But what is the evidence for it? Graetz offers none in his brilliant Commentary on Canticles. In proof of his startling view that, throughout post-Exilic times, the shepherd vocation was held in low repute among Israelites, he merely refers to an article in his Monatsschrift (1870, p. 483). When one turns to that, one finds that it concerns a far later period, the second Christian century, when the shepherd vocation had fallen to the grade of a small and disreputable trade. The vocation was then no longer a necessary corollary of the sacrificial needs of the Temple. While the altar of Jerusalem required its holocausts, the breeders of the animals would hardly have been treated as pariahs. In the century immediately following the destruction of the Temple, the shepherd began to fall in moral esteem, and in the next century he was included among the criminal categories. No doubt, too, as the tender of flocks was often an Arab raider, the shepherd had become a dishonest poacher on other men's preserves. The attitude towards him was, further, an outcome of the deepening antagonism between the schoolmen and the peasantry. But even then it was by no means invariable. One of the most famous of Rabbis, Akiba, who died a martyr in 135 C.E., was not only a shepherd, but he was also the hero of the most romantic of Rabbinic love episodes.

At the very time when Graetz thinks that agriculture had superseded pastoral pursuits in general esteem, the Book of Ecclesiasticus was written. On the one side, Sirach, the author of this Apocryphal work, does not hesitate (ch. xxiv) to compare his beloved Wisdom to a garden, in the same rustic images that we find in Canticles; and, on the other side, he reveals none of that elevated appreciation of agriculture which Graetz would have us expect. Sirach (xxxvii. 25) asks sarcastically:

How shall he become wise that holdeth the plough,
That glorieth in the shaft of the goad:
That driveth oxen, and is occupied with their labors,
And whose talk is of bullocks?

Here it is the farmer that is despised, not a word is hinted against the shepherd. Sirach also has little fondness for commerce, and he denies the possibility of wisdom to the artisan and craftsman, "in whose ear is ever the noise of the hammer" (ib. v. 28). Sirach, indeed, is not attacking these occupations; he regards them all as a necessary evil, "without these cannot a city be inhabited" (v. 32). Our Jerusalem savant, as Dr. Schechter well terms him, of the third or fourth century B.C.E.; is merely illustrating his thesis, that 'The wisdom of the scribe cometh by opportunity of leisure'; And he that hath little business shall become wise, or, as he puts it otherwise, sought for in the council of the people, and chosen to sit in the seat of the judge. This view finds its analogue in a famous saying of the later Jewish sage Hillel, "Not everyone who increaseth business attains wisdom" (Aboth, ii. 5).

Undeniably, the shepherd lost in dignity in the periods of Jewish prosperity and settled city life. But, as George Adam Smith points out accurately, the prevailing character of Judea is naturally pastoral, with husbandry only incidental. "Judea, indeed, offers as good ground as there is in all the East for observing the grandeur of the shepherd's character,"–his devotion, his tenderness, his opportunity of leisurely communion with nature.

The same characterization must have held in ancient times. And, after all, as Graetz himself admits, the poet of Canticles locates his shepherd in Gilead, the wild jasmine and other flowers of whose pastures (the "lilies" of the Song) still excite the admiration of travellers. Laurence Oliphant is lost in delight over the "anemones, cyclamens, asphodels, iris," which burst on his view as he rode "knee-deep through the long, rich, sweet grass, abundantly studded with noble oak and terebinth trees," and all this in Gilead. When, then, the Hebrew poet placed his shepherd and his flocks among the lilies, he was not trying to conciliate the courtly aristocrats of Jerusalem, or reconcile them to his Theocritan conventions; he was simply drawing his picture from life.

And as to the poetical idealization of the shepherd, how could a Hebrew poet fail to idealize him, under the ever-present charm of his traditional lore, of Jacob the shepherd-patriarch, Moses the shepherd-lawgiver, David the shepherd-king, and Amos the shepherd-prophet? So God becomes the Shepherd of Israel, not only explicitly in the early twenty-third Psalm, but implicitly also, in the late 119th. The same idealization is found everywhere in the Rabbinic literature as well as in the New Testament. Moses is the hero of the beautiful Midrashic parable of the straying lamb, which he seeks in the desert, and bears in his bosom (Exodus Rabba, ii). There is, on the other hand, something topsy-turvy in Graetz's suggestion, that a Hebrew poet would go abroad for a conventional idealization of the shepherd character, just when, on his theory, pastoral conditions were scorned and lightly esteemed at home.

It was unnecessary, then, and inappropriate for the author of Canticles to go to Theocritus for the pastoral characters of his poem. But did he borrow its form and structure from the Greek? Nothing seems less akin than the slight dramatic interest of the idylls and the strong, if obscure, dramatic plot of Canticles. Budde has failed altogether to convince readers of the Song that no consistent story runs through it. It is, as has been said above, incredible that we should have before us nothing more than the disconnected ditties of a Syrian wedding-minstrel. Graetz knew nothing of the repertoire theory that has been based on Wetzstein's discoveries of modern Syrian marriage songs and dances. Graetz believed, as most still do, that Canticles is a whole, not an aggregation of parts; yet he held that, not only the dramatis personae, but the very structure of the Hebrew poem must be traced to Theocritus. He appeals, in particular, to the second Idyll of the Greek poet, wherein the lady casts her magic spells in the vain hope of recovering the allegiance of her butterfly admirer. Obviously, there is no kinship between the facile Sirnaitha of the Idyll and the difficult Shulammith of Canticles: one the seeker, the other the sought; between the sensuous, unrestrained passion of the former and the self-sacrificing, continent affection of the latter. The nobler conceptions of love derive from the Judean maiden, not from the Greek paramour. But, argues Graetz with extraordinary ingenuity, Simaitha, recounting her unfortunate love-affair, introduces, as Shulammith does, dialogues between herself and her absent lover; she repeats what he said to her, and she to him; her monologue is no more a soliloquy than are the monologues of Shulammith, for both have an audience: here Thestylis, there the chorus of women. Simaitha's second refrain, as she bewails her love, after casting the ingredients into the bowl, turning the magic wheel to draw home to her the man she loves, runs thus:

Bethink thee, mistress Moon, whence came my love!

Graetz compares this to Shulammith's refrain in Canticles:

I adjure you, O daughters of Jerusalem,
  By the roes,
  And by the hinds of the field,
That ye stir not up
Nor awaken love,
  Until it please!

But in meaning the refrains have an absolutely opposite sense, and, more than that, they have an absolutely opposite function. In the Idyll the refrain is an accompaniment, in the Song it is an intermezzo. It occurs three times (ii. 7; iii. 5; and viii. 4), and like other repeated refrains in the Song concludes a scene, marks a transition in the situation. In Theocritus refrains are links, in the Song they are breaks in the chain.

Refrains are of the essence of lyric poetry as soon as anything like narrative enters into it. They are found throughout the lyrics of the Old Testament, the Psalms providing several examples. They belong to the essence of the Hebrew strophic system. And so it is with the other structural devices to which Graetz refers: reminiscent narrative, reported dialogues, scenes within the scene–all are common features (with certain differences) of the native Hebraic style, and they supply no justification for the suggestion of borrowing from non-Hebraic models.

There have, on the other side, been many, especially among older critics, who have contended that Theocritus owed his inspiration to Canticles. These have not been disturbed by the consideration, that, if he borrowed at all, he must assuredly have borrowed more than the most generous of them assert that he did. Recently an ingenious advocate of this view has appeared in Professor D.S. Margoliouth, all of whose critical work is rich in originality and surprises. In the first chapter of his "Lines of Defence of the Biblical Revelation," he turns the tables on Graetz with quite entertaining thoroughness. Graetz was certain that no Hebrew poet could have drawn his shepherds from life; Margoliouth is equally sure that no Greek could have done so.

"That this style [bucolic poetry], in which highly artificial performances are ascribed to shepherds and cowherds, should have originated in Greece, would be surprising; for the persons who followed these callings were ordinarily slaves, or humble hirelings, whom the classical writers treat with little respect. But from the time of Theocritus their profession becomes associated with poetic art. The shepherd's clothes are donned by Virgil, Spenser, and Milton. The existence of the Greek translation of the Song of Solomon gives us the explanation of this fact. The Song of Solomon is a pastoral poem, but its pictures are true to nature. The father of the writer [Margoliouth believes in the Solomonic authorship of Canticles], himself both a king and a poet, had kept sheep. The combination of court life with country life, which in Theocritus seems so unnatural, was perfectly natural in pre-Exilic Palestine. Hence the rich descriptions of the country (ii. 12) beside the glowing descriptions of the king's wealth (iii. 10).

Theocritus can match both (Idylls vii and xv), but it may be doubted whether he could have found any Greek model for either."

It is disturbing to one's confidence in the value of Biblical criticism–both of the liberal school (Graetz) and the conservative (Margoliouth)–to come across so complete an antithesis. But things are not quite so bad as they look. Each critic is half right–Margoliouth in believing the pastoral pictures of Canticles true to Judean life, Graetz in esteeming the pastoral pictures of the Idylls true to Sicilian life. The English critic supports his theme with some philological arguments. He suggests that the vagaries of the Theocritan dialect are due to the fact that the Idyllist was a foreigner, whose native language was "probably Hebrew or Syriac." Or perhaps Theocritus used the Greek translation of the Song, "unless Theocritus himself was the translator." All of this is a capital jeu d'esprit, but it is scarcely possible that Canticles was translated into Greek so early as Theocritus, and, curiously enough, the Septuagint Greek version of the Song has less linguistic likeness to the phraseology of Theocritus than has the Greek version of the Song by a contemporary of Akiba, the proselyte Aquila. Margoliouth points out a transference by Theocritus of the word for daughter-in-law to the meaning bride (Idyll, xviii. 15). This is a Hebraism, he thinks. But expansions of meaning in words signifying relationship are common to all poets. Far more curious is a transference of this kind that Theocritus does not make. Had he known Canticles, he would surely have seized upon the Hebrew use of sister to mean beloved, a usage which, innocent and tender enough in the Hebrew, would have been highly acceptable to the incestuous patron of Theocritus, who actually married his full sister. Strange to say, the ancient Egyptian love poetry employs the terms brother and sister as regular denotations of a pair of lovers.

This last allusion to an ancient Egyptian similarity to a characteristic usage of Canticles leads to the remark, that Maspero and Spiegelberg have both published hieroglyphic poems of the xixth-xxth Dynasties, in which may be found other parallels to the metaphors and symbolism of the Hebrew Song. As earlier writers exaggerated the likeness of Canticles to Theocritus, so Maspero was at first inclined to exaggerate the affinity of Canticles to the old Egyptian amatory verse. It is not surprising, but it is saddening, to find that Maspero, summarizing his interesting discovery in 1883, used almost the same language as Lessing had used in 1777 with reference to Theocritus. Maspero, it is true, was too sane a critic to assert borrowing on the part of Canticles. But he speaks of the "same manner of speech, the same images, the same comparisons," as Lessing does. Now if A = B, and B = C, then it follows that A = C. But in this case A does not equal C. There is no similarity at all between the Egyptian Songs and Theocritus. It follows that there is no essential likeness between Canticles and either of the other two. In his later books, Maspero has tacitly withdrawn his assertion of close Egyptian similarity, and it would be well if an equally frank withdrawal were made by the advocates of a close Theocritan parallel.

Some of the suggested resemblances between the Hebrew and Greek Songs are perhaps interesting enough to be worth examining in detail. In Idyll i. 24, the goatherd offers this reward to Thyrsis, if he will but sing the song of Daphnis:

> I'll give thee first
> To milk, ay, thrice, a goat; she suckles twins,
> Yet ne'ertheless can fill two milkpails full.

It can hardly be put forward as a remarkable fact that the poet should refer to so common an incident in sheep-breeding as the birth of twins. Yet the twins have been forced into the dispute, though it is hard to conceive anything more unlike than the previous quotation and the one that follows from Canticles (iv. 2):

> Thy teeth are like a flock of ewes,
>   That are newly shorn,
>   Which are come up from the washing,
> Whereof every one hath twins,
> And none is bereaved among them.

It is doubtful whether the Hebrew knows anything at all of the twin-bearing ewes; the penultimate line ought rather to be rendered (as in the margin of the Revised Version) "thy teeth ... which are all of them in pairs." But, however rendered, the Hebrew means this. Theocritus speaks of the richness of the goat's milk, for, after having fed her twins, she has still enough milk to fill two pails. In Canticles, the maiden's teeth, spotlessly white, are smooth and even, "they run accurately in pairs, the upper corresponding to the lower, and none of them is wanting" (Harper).

Even more amusing is the supposed indebtedness on one side or the other in the reference made by Theocritus and Canticles to the ravages of foxes in vineyards. Theocritus has these beautiful lines in his first Idyll (lines 44 et seq.):

Hard by that wave-beat sire a vineyard bends
Beneath its graceful load of burnished grapes;
A boy sits on the rude fence watching them.
Near him two foxes: down the rows of grapes
One ranging steals the ripest; one assails
With wiles the poor lad's scrip, to leave him soon
Stranded and supperless. He plaits meanwhile
With ears of corn a right fine cricket-trap,
And fits it in a rush: for vines, for scrip,
Little he cares, enamored of his toy.

How different the scene in Canticles (ii. 14 et seq.) that has been quoted above!

Take us the foxes,
   The little foxes,
   That spoil the vineyards,
For our vineyards are in blossom!

Canticles alludes to the destruction of the young shoots, Theocritus pictures the foxes devouring the ripe grapes. (Comp. also Idyll v. 112.) Foxes commit both forms of depredation, but the poets have seized on different aspects of the fact. Even were the aspects identical, it would be ridiculous to suppose that the Sicilian or Judean had been guilty of plagiarism. To-day, as of old, in the vineyards of Palestine you may see the little stone huts of the watchers on the lookout for the foxes, or jackals, whose visitations begin in the late spring and continue to the autumn. In Canticles we have a genuine fragment of native Judean folk-song; in Theocritus an equally native item of every season's observation.

So with most of the other parallels. It is only necessary to set out the passages in full, to see that the similarity is insignificant in relation to the real differences. One would have thought that any poet dealing with rustic beauty might light on the fact that a sunburnt skin may be attractive. Yet Margoliouth dignifies this simple piece of observation into a theory! "The theory that swarthiness produced by sun-burning need not be disfiguring to a woman" is, Margoliouth holds, taken by Theocritus from Canticles. Graetz, as usual, reverses the relation: Canticles took it from Theocritus. But beyond the not very recondite idea that a sunburnt maid may still be charming, there is no parallel. Battus sings (Idyll x. 26 et seq.):

Fair Bombyca! thee do men report
   Lean, dusk, a gipsy: I alone nut-brown.
Violets and pencilled hyacinths are swart,
   Yet first of flowers they're chosen for a crown.
As goats pursue the clover, wolves the goat,
   And cranes the ploughman, upon thee I dote!
In Canticles the Shulammite protests (i. 5 et seq.):

I am black but comely,
   O ye daughters of Jerusalem!
[Black] as the tents of Kedar,
[Comely] as the curtains of Solomon.
   Despise me not because I am swarthy,
   Because the sun hath scorched me.
My mother's sons were incensed against me,
They made me the keeper of the vineyards,
But mine own vineyard I have not kept!

     Two exquisite lyrics these, of which it is hard to say which has been more influential as a key-note of later poetry. But neither of them is derived; each is too spontaneous, too fresh from the poet's soul.

     Before turning to one rather arrestive parallel, a word may be said on Graetz's idea, that Canticles uses the expression "love's arrows." Were this so, the symbolism could scarcely be attributed to other than a Greek original. The line occurs in the noble panegyric of love cited before, with which Canticles ends, and in which the whole drama culminates. There is no room in this eulogy for Graetz's rendering, "Her arrows are fiery arrows," nor can the Hebrew easily mean it. "The flashes thereof are flashes of fire," is the best translation possible of the Hebrew line. There is nothing Greek in the comparison of love to fire, for fire is used in common Hebrew idiom to denote any powerful emotion (comp. the association of fire with jealousy in Ezekiel xxxix. 4).

Ewald, while refusing to connect the Idylls with Canticles, admitted that one particular parallel is at first sight forcible. It is the comparison of both Helen and Shulammith to a horse. Margoliouth thinks the Greek inexplicable without the Hebrew; Graetz thinks the Hebrew inexplicable without the Greek. In point of fact, the Hebrew and the Greek do not explain each other in the least. In the Epithalamium (Idyll xviii. 30) Theocritus writes,

Or as in a chariot a mare of Thessalian breed,
So is rose-red Helen, the glory of Lacedemon.

The exact point of comparison is far from clear, but it must be some feature of beauty or grace. Such a comparison, says Margoliouth, is extraordinary in a Greek poet; he must have derived it from a non-Greek source. But it has escaped this critic and all the commentaries on Theocritus, that just this comparison is perfectly natural for a Sicilian poet, familiar with several series of Syracusan coins of all periods, on which appear chariots with Nike driving horses of the most delicate beauty, fit figures to compare to a maiden's grace of form. Theocritus, however, does not actually compare Helen to the horse; she beautifies or sets off Lacedemon as the horse sets off the chariot. Graetz, convinced that the figure is Greek, pronounces the Hebrew unintelligible without it. But it is quite appropriate to the Hebrew poet. Having identified his royal lover with Solomon, the poet was almost driven to make some allusion to Solomon's famed exploit in importing costly horses and chariots from Egypt (I Kings x. 26-29). And so Canticles says (i. 9):

I have compared thee, O my love,
To a team of horses, in Pharaoh's chariots.
Thy cheeks are comely with rows of pearls,
Thy neck with chains of gold.

The last couplet refers to the ornaments of the horse's bridle and neck. Now, to the Hebrew the horse was almost invariably associated with war. The Shulammite is elsewhere (vi. 4) termed "terrible as an army with banners." In Theocritus the comparison is primarily to Helen's beauty; in Canticles to the Shulammite's awesomeness,

Turn away thine eyes from me,
For they have made me afraid.

These foregoing points of resemblance are the most significant that have been adduced. And they are not only seen to be each unimportant and inconclusive, but they have no cumulative effect. Taken as wholes, as was said above, the Idylls and Canticles are the poles asunder in their moral attitude towards love and in their general literary treatment of the theme. Of course, poets describing the spring will always speak of the birds; Greek and Hebrew loved flowers, Jew and Egyptian heard the turtle-dove as a harbinger of nature's rebirth; sun and moon are everywhere types of warm and tender feelings; love is the converter of a winter of discontent into a glorious summer. In all love poems the wooer would fain embrace the wooed. And if she prove coy, he will tell of the menial parts he would be ready to perform, to continue unrebuked in her vicinity. Anacreon's lover (xx) would be water in which the maid should bathe, and the Egyptian sighs, "Were I but the washer of her clothes, I should breathe the scent of her." Or the Egyptian will cry, "O were I the ring on her finger, that I might be ever with her," just as the Shulammite bids her beloved (though in another sense) "Place me as a seal on thine hand" (Cant. viii. 6). Love intoxicates like wine; the maiden has a honeyed tongue; her forehead and neck are like ivory. Nothing in all this goes beyond the identity of feeling that lies behind all poetical expression. But even in this realm of metaphor and image and symbolism, the North-Semitic wasf and even more the Hebraic parallels given in other parts of the Bible are closer far. Hosea xiv. 6-9 (with its lilies, its figure of Israel growing in beauty as the olive tree, "and his smell as Lebanon"), Proverbs (with its eulogy of faithful wedded love, its lips dropping honeycomb, its picture of a bed perfumed with myrrh, aloes, and cinnamon, the wife to love whom is to drink water from one's own well, and she the pleasant roe and loving hind)–these and the royal Epithalamium (Ps. xlv), and other Biblical passages too numerous to quote, constitute the real parallels to the imagery and idealism of Canticles.

The only genuine resemblance arises from identity of environment. If Theocritus and the poet of Canticles were contemporaries, they wrote when there had been a somewhat sudden growth of town life both in Egypt and Palestine. Alexander the Great and his immediate successors were the most assiduous builders of new cities that the world has ever seen. The charms of town life made an easy conquest of the Orient. But pastoral life would not surrender without a struggle. It would, during this violent revolution in habits, reassert itself from time to time. We can suppose that after a century of experience of the delusions of urban comfort, the denizens of towns would welcome a reminder of the delights of life under the open sky. There would be a longing for something fresher, simpler, freer. At such a moment Theocritus, like the poet of Canticles, had an irresistible opportunity, and to this extent the Idylls and the Song are parallel.

But, on the other hand, when we pass from external conditions to intrinsic purport, nothing shows better the difference between Theocritus and Canticles than the fact that the Hebrew poem has been so susceptible of allegorization. Though the religious, symbolical interpretation of the Song be far from its primary meaning, yet in the Hebrew muse the sensuous and the mystical glide imperceptibly into one another. And this is true of Semitic poetry in general. It is possible to give a mystical turn to the quatrains of Omar Khayyam. But this can hardly be done with Anacreon. There is even less trace of Semitic mysticism in Theocritus than in Anacreon. Idylls and Canticles have some similarities. But these are only skin deep. In their heart of hearts the Greek and Judean poets are strangers, and so are their heroes and heroines.

No apology is needed for the foregoing lengthy discussion of the Song of Songs, seeing that it is incomparably the finest love poem in the Hebrew, or any other language. And this is true whatever be one's opinion of its primary significance. It was no doubt its sacred interpretation that imparted to it so lasting a power over religious symbolism. But its human import also entered into its eternal influence. The Greek peasants of Macedonia still sing echoes from the Hebrew song. Still may be heard, in modern Greek love chants, the sweet old phrase, "black but comely," a favorite phrase with all swarthy races; "my sister, my bride" remains as the most tender term of endearment. To a certain extent the service has been repaid. Some of the finest melodies to which the Synagogue hymns, or Piyyutim, are set, are the melodies to Achoth Ketannah, based on Canticles viii. 8, and Berach Dodi, a frequent phrase of the Hebrew book. The latter melody is similar to the finer melodies of the Levant; the former strikingly recalls the contemporary melodies of the Greek Archipelago. To turn a final glance at the other side of the indebtedness, we need only recall that Edmund Spenser's famous Marriage Ode–the Epithalamium–the noblest marriage ode in the English language, and Milton's equally famous description of Paradise in the fourth book of his Epic, owe a good deal to direct imitation of the Song of Songs. It is scarcely an exaggeration to assert that the stock-in-trade of many an erotic poet is simply the phraseology of the divine song which we have been considering so inadequately. It did not start as a repertoire; it has ended as one.

We must now make a great stride through the ages. Between the author of the Song of Songs and the next writer of inspired Hebrew love songs there stretches an interval of at least fourteen centuries. It is an oft-told story, how, with the destruction of the Temple, the Jewish desire for song temporarily ceased. The sorrow-laden heart could not sing of love. The disuse of a faculty leads to its loss; and so, with the cessation of the desire for song, the gift of singing became atrophied. But the decay was not quite complete. It is commonly assumed that post-Biblical Hebrew poetry revived for sacred ends; first hymns were written, then secular songs. But Dr. Brody has proved that this assumption is erroneous. In point of fact, the first Hebrew poetry after the Bible was secular not religious. We find in the pages of Talmud and Midrash relics and fragments of secular poetry, snatches of bridal songs, riddles, elegies, but less evidence of a religious poetry. True, when once the medieval burst of Hebrew melody established itself, the Hebrew hymns surpassed the secular Hebrew poems in originality and inspiration. But the secular verses, whether on ordinary subjects, or as addresses to famous men, and invocations on documents, at times far exceed the religious poems in range and number. And in many ways the secular poetry deserves very close attention. A language is not living when it is merely ecclesiastical. No one calls Sanskrit a living language because some Indian sects still pray in Sanskrit. But when Jewish poets took to using Hebrew again–if, indeed, they ever ceased to use it–as the language of daily life, as the medium for expressing their human emotions, then one can see that the sacred tongue was on the way to becoming once more what it is to-day in many parts of Palestine–the living tongue of men.

It must not be thought that in the Middle Ages there were two classes of Hebrew poets: those who wrote hymns and those who wrote love songs. With the exception of Solomon ibn Gabirol–a big exception, I admit–the best love songs were written by the best hymn writers. Even Ibn Gabirol, who, so far as we know, wrote no love songs, composed other kinds of secular poetry. One of the favorite poetical forms of the Middle Ages consisted of metrical letters to friends–one may almost assert that the best Hebrew love poetry is of this type–epistles of affection between man and man, expressing a love passing the love of woman. Ibn Gabirol wrote such epistles, but the fact remains that we know of no love verses from his hand; perhaps this confirms the tradition that he was the victim of an unrequited affection.

Thus the new form opens not with Ibn Gabirol, but with Samuel ibn Nagrela. He was Vizier of the Khalif, and Nagid, or Prince, of the Jews, in the eleventh century in Spain, and, besides Synagogue hymns and Talmudic treatises, he wrote love lyrics. The earlier hymns of Kalir have, indeed, a strong emotional undertone, but the Spanish school may justly claim to have created a new form. And this new form opens with Samuel the Nagid's pretty verses on his "Stammering Love," who means to deny, but stammers out assent. I cite the metrical German version of Dr. Egers, because I have found it impossible to reproduce (Dr. Egers is not very precise or happy in his attempt to reproduce) the puns of the original. The sense, however, is clear. The stammering maid's words, being mumbled, convey an invitation, when they were intended to repulse her loving admirer.

Wo ist mein stammelnd Lieb?
Wo sie, die würz'ge, blieb?
Verdunkelt der Mond der Sterne Licht,
Ueberstrahlt den Mond ihr Angesicht!
Wie Schwalbe, wie Kranich, die
Bei ihrer Ankunft girren,
Vertraut auf ihren Gott auch sie
In ihrer Zunge Irren.

Mir schmollend rief sie "Erzdieb,"
Hervor doch haucht sie "Herzdieb"–
Hin springe ich zum Herzlieb.
"Ehrloser!" statt zu wehren,
"Her, Loser!" lässt sie hören;
Nur rascher dem Begehren
Folgt' ich mit ihr zu kosen,
Die lieblich ist wie Rosen.

  This poem deserves attention, as it is one of the first, if not actually the very first, of its kind. The Hebrew poet is forsaking the manner of the Bible for the manner of the Arabs. One point of resemblance between the new Hebrew and the Arabic love poetry is obscured in the translation. In the Hebrew of Samuel the Nagid the terms of endearment, applied though they are to a girl, are all in the masculine gender. This, as Dr. Egers observes, is a common feature of the Arabic and Persian love poetry of ancient and modern times. An Arab poet will praise his fair one's face as "bearded" with garlands of lilies. Hafiz describes a girl's cheeks as roses within a net of violets, the net referring to the beard. Jehudah Halevi uses this selfsame image, and Moses ibn Ezra and the rest also employ manly figures of speech in portraying beautiful women. All this goes to show how much, besides rhyme and versification, medieval Hebrew love poetry owed to Arabic models. Here, for instance, is an Arabic poem, whose author, Radhi Billah, died in 940, that is, before the Spanish Jewish poets began to write of love. To an Arabic poet Laila replaces the Lesbia of Catullus and the Chloe of the Elizabethans. This tenth century Arabic poem runs thus:

Laila, whene'er I gaze on thee,
 My altered cheeks turn pale;
While upon thine, sweet maid, I see
 A deep'ning blush prevail.

Laila, shall I the cause impart
 Why such a change takes place?–
The crimson stream deserts my heart
 To mantle on thy face.

Here we have fully in bloom, in the tenth century, those conceits which meet us, not only in the Hebrew poets of the next two centuries, but also in the English poets of the later Elizabethan age.

It is very artificial and scarcely sincere, but also undeniably attractive. Or, again, in the lines of Zoheir, addressed by the lover to a messenger that has just brought tidings from the beloved,

Oh! let me look upon thine eyes again,
For they have looked upon the maid I love,

we have, in the thirteenth century, the very airs and tricks of the cavalier poets. In fact, it cannot be too often said that love poetry, like love itself, is human and eternal, not of a people and an age, but of all men and all times. Though fashions change in poetry as in other ornament, still the language of love has a long life, and age after age the same conceits and terms of endearment meet us. Thus Hafiz has these lines,

I praise God who made day and night:
Day thy countenance, and thy hair the night.
Long before him the Hebrew poet Abraham ibn Ezra had written,

On thy cheeks and the hair of thy head
I will bless: He formeth light and maketh darkness.

In the thirteenth century the very same witticism meets us again, in the Hebrew Machberoth of Immanuel. But obviously it would be an endless task to trace the similarities of poetic diction between Hebrew and other poets: suffice it to realize that such similarities exist.

Such similarities did not, however, arise only from natural causes. They were, in part at all events, due to artificial compulsion. It is well to bear this in mind, for the recurrence of identical images in Hebrew love poem after love poem impresses a Western reader as a defect. To the Oriental reader, on the contrary, the repetition of metaphors seemed a merit. It was one of the rules of the game. In his "Literary History of Persia" Professor Browne makes this so clear that a citation from him will save me many pages. Professor Browne (ii, 83) analyzes Sharafu'd-Din Rami's rhetorical handbook entitled the "Lover's Companion." The "Companion" legislates as to the similes and figures that may be used in describing the features of a girl.

"It contains nineteen chapters, treating respectively of the hair, the forehead, the eyebrows, the eyes, the eyelashes, the face, the down on lips and cheeks, the mole or beauty-spot, the lips, the teeth, the mouth, the chin, the neck, the bosom, the arm, the fingers, the figure, the waist, and the legs. In each chapter the author first gives the various terms applied by the Arabs and Persians to the part which he is discussing, differentiating them when any difference in meaning exists; then the metaphors used by writers in speaking of them, and the epithets applied to them, the whole copiously illustrated by examples from the poets."

No other figures of speech would be admissible. Now this "Companion" belongs to the fourteenth century, and the earlier Arabic and Persian poetry was less fettered. But principles of this kind clearly affected the Hebrew poets, and hence there arises a certain monotony in the songs, especially when they are read in translation. The monotony is not so painfully prominent in the originals. For the translator can only render the substance, and the substance is often more conventional than the nuances of form, the happy turns and subtleties, which evaporate in the process of translation, leaving only the conventional sediment behind.

This is true even of Jehudah Halevi, though in him we hear a genuinely original note. In his Synagogue hymns he joins hands with the past, with the Psalmists; in his love poems he joins hands with the future, with Heine. His love poetry is at once dainty and sincere. He draws indiscriminately on Hebrew and Arabic models, but he is no mere imitator. I will not quote much from him, for his best verses are too familiar. Those examples which I must present are given in a new and hitherto unpublished translation by Mrs. Lucas.

Marriage Song
  Fair is my dove, my loved one,
    None can with her compare:
  Yea, comely as Jerusalem,
    Like unto Tirzah fair.

Shall she in tents unstable
  A wanderer abide,
While in my heart awaits her
  A dwelling deep and wide?

The magic of her beauty
  Has stolen my heart away:
Not Egypt's wise enchanters
  Held half such wondrous sway.

E'en as the changing opal
  In varying lustre glows,
Her face at every moment
  New charms and sweetness shows.

White lilies and red roses
  There blossom on one stem:
Her lips of crimson berries
  Tempt mine to gather them.

By dusky tresses shaded
  Her brow gleams fair and pale,
Like to the sun at twilight,
  Behind a cloudy veil.

Her beauty shames the day-star,
  And makes the darkness light:
Day in her radiant presence
  Grows seven times more bright

This is a lonely lover!
  Come, fair one, to his side,
That happy be together
  The bridegroom and the bride!

The hour of love approaches
  That shall make one of twain:
Soon may be thus united
  All Israel's hosts again!
OPHRAH

To her sleeping Love

> Awake, my fair, my love, awake,
>   That I may gaze on thee!
> And if one fain to kiss thy lips
>   Thou in thy dreams dost see,
> Lo, I myself then of thy dream
>   The interpreter will be!

TO OPHRAH

> Ophrah shall wash her garments white
>   In rivers of my tears,
> And dry them in the radiance bright
>   That shines when she appears.
> Thus will she seek no sun nor water nigh,
> Her beauty and mine eyes will all her needs supply.

    These lovers' tears often meet us in the Hebrew poems. Ibn Gabirol speaks of his tears as fertilizing his heart and preserving it from crumbling into dust. Mostly, however, the Hebrew lover's tears, when they are not tokens of grief at the absence of the beloved, are the involuntary confession of the man's love. It is the men who must weep in these poems. Charizi sings of the lover whose heart succeeds in concealing its love, whose lips contrive to maintain silence on the subject, but his tears play traitor and betray his affection to all the world. Dr. Sulzbach aptly quotes parallels to this fancy from Goethe and Brentano.

    This suggestion of parallelism between a medieval Hebrew poet and Goethe must be my excuse for an excursion into what seems to me one of the most interesting examples of the kind. In one of his poems Jehudah Halevi has these lines:

Separation
> So we must be divided! Sweetest, stay!
>   Once more mine eyes would seek thy glance's light!
> At night I shall recall thee; thou, I pray,
>   Be mindful of the days of our delight!
> Come to me in my dreams, I ask of thee,
> And even in thy dreams be gentle unto me!

> If thou shouldst send me greeting in the grave,
>   The cold breath of the grave itself were sweet;
> Oh, take my life! my life, 'tis all I have,
>   If I should make thee live I do entreat!
> I think that I shall hear, when I am dead,
>   The rustle of thy gown, thy footsteps overhead.

It is this last image that has so interesting a literary history as to tempt me into a digression. But first a word must be said of the translation and the translator. The late Amy Levy made this rendering, not from the Hebrew, but from Geiger's German with obvious indebtedness to Emma Lazarus. So excellent, however, was Geiger's German that Miss Levy got quite close to the meaning of the original, though thirty-eight Hebrew lines are compressed into twelve English. Literally rendered, the Hebrew of the last lines runs:

> Would that, when I am dead, to mine ears may rise
> The music of the golden bell upon thy skirts.

This image of the bell is purely Hebraic; it is, of course, derived from the High Priest's vestments. Jehudah Halevi often employs it to express melodious proclamation of virtue, or the widely-borne voice of fame. Here he uses it in another context, and though the image of the bell is not repeated, yet some famous lines from Tennyson's "Maud" at once come into one's mind:

> She is coming, my own, my sweet;
>   Were it ever so light a tread,
> My heart would hear her and beat,
>   Were it earth in an earthy bed;
> My dust would hear her and beat,
>   Had I lain for a century dead;
> Would start and tremble under her feet,
>   And blossom in purple and red.

It is thus that the lyric poetry of one age affects, or finds its echo in, that of another, but in this particular case it is, of course, a natural thought that true love must survive the grave. There is a mystical union between the two souls, which death cannot end. Here, again, we meet the close connection between love and mysticism, which lies at the root of all deep love poetry. But we must attend to the literary history of the thought for a moment longer. Moses ibn Ezra, though more famous for his Synagogue hymns, had some lyric gifts of a lighter touch, and he wrote love songs on occasion. In one of these the poet represents a dying wife as turning to her husband with the pathetic prayer, "Remember the covenant of our youth, and knock at the door of my grave with a hand of love."

I will allude only to one other parallel, which carries us to a much earlier period. Here is an Arab song of Taubah, son of Al-Humaiyir, who lived in the seventh century. It must be remembered that it was an ancient Arabic folk-idea that the spirits of the dead became owls.

> Ah, if but Laila would send me a greeting down
>   of grace, though between us lay the dust and flags of stone,
> My greeting of joy should spring in answer, or there should cry
>   toward her an owl, ill bird that shrieks in the gloom of graves.

C.J.L. Lyall, writing of the author of these lines, Taubah, informs us that he was the cousin of Laila, a woman of great beauty. Taubah had loved her when they were children in the desert together, but her father refused to give her to him in marriage. He led a stormy life, and met his death in a fight during the reign of Mu'awiyah. Laila long survived him, but never forgot him or his love for her. She attained great fame as a poetess, and died during the reign of 'Abd-al-Malik, son of Marwan, at an advanced age. "A tale is told of her death in which these verses figure. She was making a journey with her husband when they passed by the grave of Taubah. Laila, who was travelling in a litter, cried, By God! I will not depart hence till I greet Taubah. Her husband endeavored to dissuade her, but she would not hearken; so at last he allowed her. And she had her camel driven up the mound on which the tomb was, and said, Peace to thee, O Taubah! Then she turned her face to the people and said, I never knew him to speak falsely until this day. What meanest thou? said they. Was it not he, she answered, who said

> Ah, if but Laila would send a greeting down
>   of grace, though between us lay the dust and flags of stone,
> My greeting of joy should spring in answer, or there should cry
>   toward her an owl, ill bird that shrieks in the gloom of graves.

Nay, but I have greeted him, and he has not answered as he said. Now, there was a she-owl crouching in the gloom by the side of the grave; and when it saw the litter and the crowd of people, it was frightened and flew in the face of the camel. And the camel was startled and cast Laila headlong on the ground; and she died that hour, and was buried by the side of Taubah."

The fascination of such parallels is fatal to proportion in an essay such as this. But I cannot honestly assert that I needed the space for other aspects of my subject. I have elsewhere fully described the Wedding Odes which Jehudah Halevi provided so abundantly, and which were long a regular feature of every Jewish marriage. But, after the brilliant Spanish period, Hebrew love songs lose their right to high literary rank. Satires on woman's wiles replace praises of her charms. On the other hand, what of inspiration the Hebrew poet felt in the erotic field beckoned towards mysticism. In the paper which opens this volume, I have written sufficiently and to spare of the woman-haters. At Barcelona, in the age of Zabara, Abraham ibn Chasdai did the best he could with his misogynist material, but he could get no nearer to a compliment than this, "Her face has the shimmer of a lamp, but it burns when held too close" ("Prince and Dervish," ch. xviii). The Hebrew attacks on women are clever, but superficial; they show no depth of insight into woman's character, and are far less effective than Pope's satires.

The boldest and ablest Hebrew love poet of the satirical school is Immanuel of Rome, a younger contemporary of Dante. He had wit, but not enough of it to excuse his ribaldry. He tells many a light tale of his amours; a pretty face is always apt to attract him and set his pen scribbling. As with the English dramatists of the Restoration, virtue and beauty are to Immanuel almost contradictory terms. For the most part, wrinkled old crones are the only decent women in his pages. His pretty women have morals as easy as the author professes. In the second of his Machberoth he contrasts two girls, Tamar and Beriah; on the one he showers every epithet of honor, at the other he hurls every epithet of abuse, only because Tamar is pretty, and Beriah the reverse. Tamar excites the love of the angels, Beriah's face makes even the devil fly. This disagreeable pose of Immanuel was not confined to his age; it has spoilt some of the best work of W.S. Gilbert. The following is Dr. Chotzner's rendering of one of Immanuel's lyrics. He entitles it

Paradise and Hell
  At times in my spirit I fitfully ponder,
    Where shall I pass after death from this light;
  Do Heaven's bright glories await me, I wonder,
    Or Lucifer's kingdom of darkness and night?

In the one, though 'tis perhaps of ill reputation,
  A crowd of gay damsels will sit by my side;
But in Heaven there's boredom and mental starvation,
  To hoary old men and old crones I'll be tied.

And so I will shun the abodes of the holy,
  And fly from the sky, which is dull, so I deem:
Let hell be my dwelling; there is no melancholy,
  Where love reigns for ever and ever supreme.

    Immanuel, it is only just to point out, occasionally draws a worthier character. In his third Machbereth he tells of a lovely girl, who is intelligent, modest, chaste, coy, and difficult, although a queen in beauty; she is simple in taste, yet exquisite in poetical feeling and musical gifts. The character is the nearest one gets in Hebrew to the best heroines of the troubadours. Immanuel and she exchange verses, but the path of flirtation runs rough. They are parted, she, woman-like, dies, and he, man-like, sings an elegy.

Even more to Immanuel's credit is his praise of his own wife. She has every womanly grace of body and soul. On her he showers compliments from the Song of Songs and the Book of Proverbs. If this be the true man revealed, then his light verses of love addressed to other women must be, as I have hinted, a mere pose. It may be that his wife read his verses, and that his picture of her was calculated to soothe her feelings when reading some other parts of his work. If she did read them, she found only one perfect figure of womanliness in her husband's poems, and that figure herself. But on the whole one is inclined to think that Immanuel's braggartism as to his many love affairs is only another aspect of the Renaissance habit, which is exemplified so completely in the similar boasts of Benvenuto Cellini.

Be this as it may, it is not surprising to find that in the Shulchan Aruch (Orach Chayyim, ch. 317, Section 16), the poems of Immanuel are put upon the Sabbath Index. It is declared unlawful to read them on Saturdays, and also on week-days, continues the Code with gathering anger. Those who copy them, still more those who print them, are declared sinners that make others to sin. I must confess that I am here on the side of the Code. Immanuel's Machberoth are scarcely worthy of the Hebrew genius.

There has been, it may be added, a long struggle against Hebrew love songs. Maimonides says ("Guide," iii. 7): "The gift of speech which God gave us to help us learn and teach and perfect ourselves–this gift of speech must not be employed in doing what is degrading and disgraceful. We must not imitate the songs and tales of ignorant and lascivious people. It may be suitable to them, but it is not fit for those who are bidden, Ye shall be a holy nation." In 1415 Solomon Alami uses words on this subject that will lead me to my last point. Alami says, "Avoid listening to love songs which excite the passions. If God has graciously bestowed on you the gift of a sweet voice, use it in praising Him. Do not set prayers to Arabic tunes, a practice which has been promoted to suit the taste of effeminate men."

But if this be a crime, then the worst offender was none other than the famous Israel Najara. In the middle of the sixteenth century he added some of its choicest lyrics to the Hebrew song-book. The most popular of the table hymns (Zemiroth) are his. He was a mystic, filled with a sense of the nearness of God. But he did not see why the devil should have all the pretty tunes. So he deliberately wrote religious poems in metres to suit Arabic, Turkish, Greek, Spanish, and Italian melodies, his avowed purpose being to divert the young Jews of his day from profane to sacred song. But these young Jews must have been exigent, indeed, if they failed to find in Najara's sacred verses enough of love and passion. Not only was he, like Jehudah Halevi, a prolific writer of Wedding Odes, but in his most spiritual hymns he uses the language of love as no Hebrew poet before or after him has done. Starting with the assumption that the Song of Songs was an allegory of God's espousal with the bride Israel, Najara did not hesitate to put the most passionate words of love for Israel into God's mouth. He was strongly attacked, but the saintly mystic Isaac Luria retorted that Najara's hymns were listened to with delight in Heaven–and if ever a man had the right to speak of Heaven it was Luria. And Hebrew poetry has no need to be ashamed of the passionate affection poured out by these mystic poets on another beloved, the Queen Sabbath.

This is not the place to speak of the Hebrew drama and of the form which the love interest takes in it. Woman, at all events, is treated far more handsomely in the dramas than in the satires. The love scenes of the Hebrew dramatists are pure to coldness. These dramas began to flourish in the eighteenth century; Luzzatto was by no means an unworthy imitator of Guarini. Sometimes the syncretism of ideas in Hebrew plays is sufficiently grotesque. Samuel Romanelli, who wrote in Italy at the era of the French Revolution, boldly introduces Greek mythology. It may be that in the Spanish period Hebrew poets introduced the muses under the epithet "daughters of Song." But with Romanelli, the classical machinery is more clearly audible. The scene of his drama is laid in Cyprus; Venus and Cupid figure in the action. Romanelli gives a moral turn to his mythology, by interposing Peace to stay the conflict between Love and Fame. Ephraim Luzzatto, at the same period, tried his hand, not unsuccessfully, at Hebrew love sonnets.

Love songs continued to be written in Hebrew in the nineteenth century, and often see the light in the twentieth. But I do not propose to deal with these. Recent new-Hebrew poetry has shown itself strongest in satire and elegy. Its note is one of anger or of pain. Shall we, however, say of the Hebrew race that it has lost the power to sing of love? Has it grown too old, too decrepid?

> And said I that my limbs were old,
> And said I that my blood was cold,
> And that my kindly fire was fled,
> And my poor withered heart was dead,
> And that I might not sing of love?

Heine is the answer. But Heine did not write in Hebrew, and those who have so far written in Hebrew are not Heines. It is, I think, vain to look to Europe for a new outburst of Hebrew love lyrics. In the East, and most of all in Palestine, where Hebrew is coming to its own again, and where the spring once more smiles on the eyes of Jewish peasants and shepherds, there may arise another inspired singer to give us a new Song of Songs in the language of the Bible. But we have no right to expect it. Such a rare thing of beauty cannot be repeated. It is a joy forever, and a joy once for all.

A Handful of Curiosities

I. George Eliot and Solomon Maimon

That George Eliot was well acquainted with certain aspects of Jewish history, is fairly clear from her writings. But there is collateral evidence of an interesting kind that proves the same fact quite conclusively, I think.

It will be remembered that Daniel Deronda went into a second-hand book-shop and bought a small volume for half a crown, thereby making the acquaintance of Ezra Cohen. Some time back I had in my hands the identical book that George Eliot purchased which formed the basis of the incident. The book may now be seen in Dr. Williams's Library, Gordon Square, London. The few words in which George Eliot dismisses the book in her novel would hardly lead one to gather how carefully and conscientiously she had read the volume, which has since been translated into English by Dr. J. Clark Murray. She, of course, bought and read the original German.

The book is Solomon Maimon's Autobiography, a fascinating piece of self-revelation and of history. (An admirable account of it may be found in chapter x of the fifth volume of the English translation of Graetz's "History of the Jews.") Maimon, cynic and skeptic, was a man all head and no heart, but he was not without "character," in one sense of the word. He forms a necessary link in the progress of modern Jews towards their newer culture. Schiller and Goethe admired him considerably, and, as we shall soon see, George Eliot was a careful student of his celebrated pages. Any reader who takes the book up, will hardly lay it down until he has finished the first part, at least.

Several marginal and other notes in the copy of the Autobiography that belonged to George Eliot are, I am convinced, in her own handwriting, and I propose to print here some of her jottings, all of which are in pencil, but carefully written. Above the Introduction, she writes: "This book might mislead many readers not acquainted with other parts of Jewish history. But for a worthy account (in brief) of Judaism and Rabbinism, see p. 150." This reference takes one to the fifteenth chapter of the Autobiography. Indeed, George Eliot was right as to the misleading tendency of a good deal in Maimon's "wonderful piece of autobiography," as she terms the work in "Daniel Deronda." She returns to the attack on p. 36 of her copy, where she has jotted, "See infra, p. 150 et seq. for a better-informed view of Talmudic study."

How carefully George Eliot read! The pagination of 207 is printed wrongly as 160; she corrects it! She corrects Kimesi into "Kimchi" on p. 48, Rabasse into "R. Ashe" on p. 163. On p. 59 she writes, "According to the Talmud no one is eternally damned." Perhaps her statement needs some slight qualification. Again (p. 62), "Rashi, i.e. Rabbi Shelomoh ben Isaak, whom Buxtorf mistakenly called Jarchi." It was really to Raymund Martini that this error goes back. But George Eliot could not know it. On p. 140, Maimon begins, "Accordingly, I sought to explain all this in the following way," to which George Eliot appends the note, "But this is simply what the Cabbala teaches–not his own ingenious explanation."

It is interesting to find George Eliot occasionally defending Judaism against Maimon. On p. 165 he talks of the "abuse of Rabbinism," in that the Rabbis tacked on new laws to old texts. "Its origin," says George Eliot's pencilled jotting, "was the need for freedom to modify laws"–a fine remark. On p. 173, where Maimon again talks of the Rabbinical method of evolving all sorts of moral truths by the oddest exegesis, she writes, "The method has been constantly pursued in various forms by Christian Teachers." On p. 186 Maimon makes merry at the annulment of vows previous to the Day of Atonement. George Eliot writes, "These are religious vows–not engagements between man and man."

Furthermore, she makes some translations of the titles of Hebrew books cited, and enters a correction of an apparently erroneous statement of fact on p. 215. There Maimon writes as though the Zohar had been promulgated after Sabbatai Zebi. George Eliot notes: "Sabbatai Zebi lived long after the production of the Zohar. He was a contemporary of Spinoza. Moses de Leon belonged to the fourteenth century." This remark shows that George Eliot knew Graetz's History, for it is he who brought the names of Spinoza and Sabbatai Zebi together in two chapter headings in his work. Besides, Graetz's History was certainly in George Eliot's library; it was among the Lewes books now at Dr.

Williams's. Again, on p. 265, Maimon speaks of the Jewish fast that falls in August. George Eliot jots on the margin, "July? Fast of Ninth Ab."

Throughout passages are pencilled, and at the end she gives an index to the parts that seem to have interested her particularly. This is her list:

>   Talmudic quotations, 36.
>   Polish Doctor, 49.
>   The Talmudist, 60.
>   Prince R. and the Barber, 110.
>   Talmudic Method, 174.
>   Polish Jews chiefly Gelehrte, 211.
>   Zohar, 215.
>   Rabbinical Morality, 176.
>   New Chasidim, 207.
>   Elias aus Wilna, 242.
>   Angels (?), 82.
>   Tamuz, II., 135.

It is a pleasure, indeed, to find a fresh confirmation, that George Eliot's favorable impression of Judaism was based on a very adequate acquaintance with its history. Sir Walter Scott's knowledge of it was, one cannot but feel, far less intimate than George Eliot's, but his poetic insight kept him marvellously straight in his appreciation of Jewish life and character.

II. How Milton Pronounced Hebrew

English politics in the seventeenth and eighteenth centuries maintained a closer association with literature than is conceivable in the present age. England has just witnessed a contest on fundamental issues between the two Houses of Parliament. This recalls, by contrast rather than by similarity, another conflict that divided the Lords from the Commons in and about the year 1645. The question at issue then was the respective literary merits of two metrical translations of the Psalms.

Francis Rous was a Provost of Eton, a member of the Westminster Assembly of Divines, and representative of Truro in the Long Parliament. This "old illiterate Jew," as Wood abusively termed him, had made a verse translation of the Psalms, which the House of Commons cordially recommended. The House of

Lords, on the other hand, preferred Barton's translation, and many other contemporaneous attempts were made to meet the growing demand for a good metrical rendering–a demand which, by the way, has remained but imperfectly filled to the present time. Would that some Jewish poet might arise to give us the long-desired version for use, at all events, in our private devotions! In April, 1648, Milton tried his hand at a rendering of nine Psalms (lxxx.-lxxxviii.), and it is from this work that we can see how Milton pronounced Hebrew. Strange to say, Milton's attempt, except in the case of the eighty-fourth Psalm, has scanty poetical merit, and, as a literal translation, it is not altogether successful. He prides himself on the fact that his verses are such that "all, but what is in a different character, are the very words of the Text, translated from the original." The inserted words in italics are, nevertheless, almost as numerous as the roman type that represents the original Hebrew. Such conventional mistakes as Rous's cherubims are, however, conspicuously absent from Milton's more scholarly work. Milton writes cherubs.

Now, in the margin of Psalms lxxx., lxxxi., lxxxii., and lxxxiii., Milton inserts a transliteration of some of the words of the original Hebrew text. The first point that strikes one is the extraordinary accuracy of the transliteration. One word appears as Jimmotu, thus showing that Milton appreciated the force of the dagesh. Again, Shiphtu-dal, bag-nadath-el show that Milton observed the presence of the Makkef. Actual mistakes are very rare, and, as Dr. Davidson has suggested, they may be due to misprints. This certainly accounts for Tishphetu instead of Tishpetu (lxxxii. 2), but when we find Be Sether appearing as two words instead of one, the capital S is rather against this explanation, while Shifta (in the last verse of Psalm lxxxii.) looks like a misreading.

It is curious to see that Milton adopted the nasal intonation of the Ayin. And he adopted it in the least defensible form. He invariably writes gn for the Hebrew Ayin. Now ng is bad enough, but gn seems a worse barbarism. Milton read the vowels, as might have been expected from one living after Reuchlin, who introduced the Italian pronunciation to Christian students in Europe, in the "Portuguese" manner, even to the point of making little, if any, distinction between the Zere and the Sheva. As to the consonants, he read Tav as th, Teth as t, Qof as k, and Vav and

Beth equally as v. In this latter point he followed the "German" usage. The letter Cheth Milton read as ch, but Kaf he read as c, sounded hard probably, as so many English readers of Hebrew do at the present day. I have even noted among Jewish boys an amusing affectation of inability to pronounce the Kaf in any other way. The somewhat inaccurate but unavoidable ts for Zadde was already established in Milton's time, while the letter Yod appears regularly as j, which Milton must have sounded as y. On the whole, it is quite clear that Milton read his Hebrew with minute precision. To see how just this verdict is, let anyone compare Milton's exactness with the erratic and slovenly transliterations in Edmund Chidmead's English edition of Leon Modena's Riti Ebraici, which was published only two years later than Milton's paraphrase of the Psalms.

The result, then, of an examination of the twenty-six words thus transliterated, is to deepen the conviction that the great Puritan poet, who derived so much inspiration from the Old Testament, drew at least some of it from the pure well of Hebrew undefiled.

III. The Cambridge Platonists

As a "Concluding Part" to "The Myths of Plato," Professor J.A. Stewart wrote a chapter on the Cambridge Platonists of the seventeenth century, his object being to show that the thought of Plato "has been, and still is, an important influence in modern philosophy."

It was a not unnatural reaction that diverted the scholars of the Renaissance from Aristotle to Plato. The medieval Church had been Aristotelian, and "antagonism to the Roman Church had, doubtless, much to do with the Platonic revival, which spread from Italy to Cambridge." But, curiously enough, the Plato whom Cambridge served was not Plato the Athenian dialectician, but Plato the poet and allegorist. It was, in fact, Philo, the Jew, rather than Plato, the Greek, that inspired them.

"Philo never thought of doubting that Platonism and the Jewish Scriptures had real affinity to each other, and hardly perhaps asked himself how the affinity was to be accounted for." Philo, however, would have had no difficulty in accounting for it; already in his day the quaint theory was prevalent that Athens had borrowed its wisdom from Jerusalem. The Cambridge Platonists went with Philo in declaring Plato to be "the Attic Moses." Henry More (1662) maintained strongly Plato's indebtedness to Moses; even Pythagoras was so indebted, or, rather, "it was a common fame [report] that Pythagoras was a disciple of the Prophet Ezekiel." The Cambridge Platonists were anxious, not only to show this dependence of Greek upon Hebraic thought, but they went on to argue that Moses taught, in allegory, the natural philosophy of Descartes. More calls Platonism the soul, and Cartesianism the body, of his own philosophy, which he applies to the explanation of the Law of Moses. "This philosophy is the old Jewish-Pythagorean Cabbala, which teaches the motion of the Earth and Pre-existence of the Soul." But it is awkward that Moses does not teach the motion of the earth. More is at no loss; he boldly argues that, though "the motion of the earth has been lost and appears not in the remains of the Jewish Cabbala, this can be no argument against its once having been a part thereof." He holds it as "exceedingly probable" that the Roman Emperor "Numa was both descended from the Jews and imbued with the Jewish religion and learning."

Thus the Cambridge Platonists of the seventeenth century are a very remarkable example of the recurrent influence exercised on non-Jews by certain forms of Judaism that had but slight direct effect on the Jews themselves. Indirectly, the Hellenic side of Jewish culture left its mark, especially in the Cabbala. It would be well worth the while of a Jewish theologian to make a close study of the seventeenth century alumni of Cambridge, who were among the most fascinating devotees of ancient Jewish wisdom. Henry More was particularly attractive, "the most interesting and the most unreadable of the whole band." When he was a young boy, his uncle had to threaten a flogging to cure him of precocious "forwardness in philosophizing concerning the mysteries of necessity and freewill." In 1631 he entered Christ's College, Cambridge, "about the time when John Milton was leaving it," and he may almost be said to have spent the rest of his life within the walls of the college, "except when he went to stay with his 'heroine pupil,' Anne, Viscountess Conway, at her country seat of Ragley in Warwickshire, where his pleasure was to wander among the woods and glades." He absolutely refused all preferment, and when "he was once persuaded to make a journey to Whitehall, to kiss His Majesty's hands, but heard by the way that this would be the prelude to a bishopric, he at once turned back." Yet More was no recluse. "He had many pupils at Christ's; he loved music, and used to play on the theorbo; he enjoyed a game at bowls, and still more a conversation with intimate friends, who listened to him as to an oracle; and he was so kind to the poor that it was said his very chamber-door was a hospital for the needy." But enough has been quoted from Overton's biography to whet curiosity about this Cambridge sage and saint. More well illustrates what was said above (pp. 114-116)–the man of letters is truest to his calling when he has at the same time an open ear to the call of humanity.

IV. The Anglo-Jewish Yiddish Literary Society

The founder and moving spirit of this unique little Society is Miss Helena Frank, whose sympathy with Yiddish literature has been shown in several ways. Her article in the Nineteenth Century ("The Land of Jargon," October, 1904) was as forcible as it was dainty. Her rendering of the stories of Perez, too, is more than a literary feat. Her knowledge of Yiddish is not merely intellectual; though not herself a Jewess, she evidently enters into the heart of the people who express their lives and aspirations in Yiddish terms. Young as she is, Miss Frank is, indeed, a remarkable linguist; Hebrew and Russian are among her accomplishments. But it is a wonderful fact that she has set herself to acquire these other languages only to help her to understand Yiddish, which latter she knows through and through.

Miss Frank not long ago founded a Society called by the title that heads this note. The Society did not interest itself directly in the preservation of Yiddish as a spoken language. It was rather the somewhat grotesque fear that the rôle of Yiddish as a living language may cease that appealed to Miss Frank. The idea was to collect a Yiddish library, encourage the translation of Yiddish books into English, and provide a sufficient supply of Yiddish books and papers for the patients in the London and other Hospitals who are unable to read any other language. The weekly Yiddishe Gazetten (New York) was sent regularly to the London Hospital, where it has been very welcome.

In the Society's first report, which I was permitted to see, Miss Frank explained why an American Yiddish paper was the first choice. In the first place, it was a good paper, with an established reputation, and at once conservative and free from prejudice. America is, moreover, "intensely interesting to the Polish Yid. For him it is the free country par excellence. Besides, he is sure to have a son, uncle, or brother there–or to be going there himself. 'Vin shterben in vin Amerika kän sich keener nisht araus drehn!' ('From dying and from going to America, there is no escape!')" Miss Frank has a keen sense of humor. How could she love Yiddish were it not so? She cites some of the Yiddishe Gazetten's answers to correspondents. This is funny: "The woman has the right to take her clothes and ornaments away with her when she leaves her husband. But it is a question if she ought to leave him." Then we have the following from an article by Dr. Goidorof. He compares the Yiddish language to persons whose passports are not in order–the one has no grammar, the others have no land.

And both the Jewish language and the Jewish nation hide their faulty passports in their wallets, and disappear from the register of nations and languages–no land, no grammar!

"A pretty conclusion the savants have come to!" (began the Jewish nation). "You are nothing but a collection of words, and I am nothing but a collection of people, and there's an end to both of us!"

"And Jargon, besides, they said–to which of us did they refer? To me or to you?" (asks the Jewish language, the word jargon being unknown to it).

"To you!" (answers the Jewish nation).

"No, to you!" (protests the Jewish language).

"Well, then, to both of us!" (allows the Jewish nation). "It seems we are both a kind of Jargon. Mercy on us, what shall we do without a grammar and without a land?"

"Unless the Zionists purchase a grammar of the Sultan!" (romances the Jewish language).

"Or at all events a land!" (sighs the Jewish nation).

"You think that the easier of the two?" (asks the Jewish language, wittily).

And at the same moment they look at one another and laugh loudly and merrily.

This is genuine Heinesque humor.

V. The Mystics and Saints of India

A book by Professor J.C. Oman, published not long ago, contains a clear and judicially sympathetic account of Hinduism. The sordid side of Indian asceticism receives due attention; the excesses of self-mortification, painful posturings, and equally painful impostures are by no means slurred over by the writer. And yet the essential origin of these ascetic practices is perceived by Professor Oman to be a pure philosophy and a not ignoble idealism. And if Professor Oman's analysis be true, one understands how it is that, though there have always been Jewish ascetics, at times of considerable numbers and devotion, yet asceticism, as such, has no recognized place in Judaism. Jewish moralists, especially, though not exclusively, those of the mystical or Cabbalistic schools, pronounce powerfully enough against over-indulgence in all sensuous pleasures; they inculcate moderation and abstinence, and, in some cases, where the pressure of desire is very strong, prescribe painful austerities, which may be paralleled by what Professor Oman tells us of the Sadhus and Yogis of India. But let us first listen to Professor Oman's analysis (p. 16):

"Without any pretence of an exhaustive analysis of the various and complex motives which underlie religious asceticism, I may, before concluding this chapter, draw attention to what seem to me the more general reasons which prompt men to ascetic practices: (1) A desire, which is intensified by all personal or national troubles, to propitiate the Unseen Powers. (2) A longing on the part of the intensely religious to follow in the footsteps of their Master, almost invariably an ascetic. (3) A wish to work out one's own future salvation, or emancipation, by conquering the evil inherent in human nature, i.e. the flesh. (4) A yearning to prepare oneself by purification of mind and body for entering into present communion with the Divine Being. (5) Despair arising from disillusionment and from defeat in the battle of life. And lastly, mere vanity, stimulated by the admiration which the multitude bestow on the ascetic."

With regard to his second reason, we find nothing of the kind in Judaism subsequent to the Essenes, until we reach the Cabbalistic heroes of the Middle Ages. The third and the fourth have, on the other hand, had power generally in Jewish conduct. The fifth has had its influence, but only temporarily and temperately. Ascetic practices, based on national and religious calamity, have, for the most part, been prescribed only for certain dates in the calendar, but it must be confessed that an excessive addiction to fasting prevails among many Jews. But it is when we consider the first of Professor Oman's reasons for ascetic practices that we perceive how entirely the genius of Judaism is foreign to Hindu and most other forms of asceticism. To reach communion with God, the Jew goes along the road of happiness, not of austerity. He serves with joy, not with sadness. On this subject the reader may refer with great profit to the remarks made by the Reverend Morris Joseph, in "Judaism as Creed and Life," p. 247, onwards, and again the whole of chapter iv. of book iii. (p. 364). Self-development, not self-mortification, is the true principle; man's lower nature is not to be crushed by torture, but to be elevated by moderation, so as to bear its part with man's higher nature in the service of God.

What leads some Jewish moralists to eulogize asceticism is that there is always a danger of the happiness theory leading to a materialistic view of life. This is what Mr. Joseph says, and says well, on the subject (p. 371):

"And, therefore, though Judaism does not approve of the ascetic temper, it is far from encouraging the materialist's view of life. It has no place for monks or hermits, who think they can serve God best by renouncing the world; but, on the other hand, it sternly rebukes the worldliness that knows no ideal but sordid pleasures, no God but Self. It commends to us the golden mean–the safe line of conduct that lies midway between the rejection of earthly joys and the worship of them. If asceticism too often spurns the commonplace duties of life, excessive self-indulgence unfits us for them. In each case we lose some of our moral efficiency. But in the latter case there is added an inevitable degradation. The man who mortifies his body for his soul's sake has at least his motive to plead for him. But the sensualist has no such justification. He deliberately chooses the evil and rejects the good. Forfeiting his character as a son of God, he yields himself a slave to unworthy passions.

"It is the same with the worldly man, who lives only for sordid ends, such as wealth and the pleasures it buys. He, too, utterly misses his vocation. His pursuit of riches may be moral in itself; he may be a perfectly honest man. But his life is unmoral all the same, for it aims at nothing higher than itself."

Thus Professor Oman's fascinating book gives occasion for thought to many whose religion is far removed from Hinduism. But there is in particular one feature of Hindu asceticism that calls for attention. This is the Hindu doctrine of Karma, or good works, which will be familiar to readers of Rudyard Kipling's "Kim." Upon a man's actions (Karma is the Sanskrit for action) in this life depends the condition in which his soul will be reincarnated.

"In a word, the present state is the result of past actions, and the future depends upon the present. Now, the ultimate hope of the Hindu should be so to live that his soul may be eventually freed from the necessity of being reincarnated, and may, in the end, be reunited to the Infinite Spirit from which it sprang. As, however, that goal is very remote, the Hindu not uncommonly limits his desire and his efforts to the attainment of a 'good time' now, and in his next appearance upon this earthly stage" (p. 108).

We need not go fully into this doctrine, which, as the writer says elsewhere (p. 172), "certainly makes for morality," but we may rather attend to that aspect of it which is shown in the Hindu desire to accumulate "merits." The performance of penances gives the self-torturer certain spiritual powers. Professor Oman quotes this passage from Sir Monier Williams's "Indian Epic Poetry" (note to p. 4):

"According to Hindu theory, the performance of penances was like making deposits in the bank of Heaven. By degrees an enormous credit was accumulated, which enabled the depositor to draw on the amount of his savings, without fear of his drafts being refused payment. The power gained in this way by weak mortals was so enormous that gods, as well as men, were equally at the mercy of these all but omnipotent ascetics, and it is remarkable that even the gods are described as engaging in penances and austerities, in order, it may be presumed, not to be undone by human beings."

Now, if for penance we substitute Mitzvoth, we find in this passage almost the caricature of the Jewish theory that meets us in the writings of German theologians. These ill-equipped critics of Judaism put it forward seriously that the Jew performs Mitzvoth in order to accumulate merit (Zechuth), and some of them even go so far as to assert that the Jew thinks of his Zechuth as irresistible. But when the matter is put frankly and squarely, as Professor Monier Williams puts it, not even the Germans could have the effrontery to assert that Judaism teaches or tolerates any such doctrine. Whatever man does, he has no merit towards God: that is Jewish teaching. Yet conduct counts, and somehow the good man and the bad man are not in the same case. Judaism may be inconsistent, but it is certainly not base in its teaching as to conduct and retribution. "Be not as servants who minister in the hope of receiving reward"-this is not the highest level of Jewish doctrine, it is the average level. Lately I have been reading a good deal of mystical Jewish literature, and I have been struck by the repeated use made of the famous Rabbinical saying of Antigonos of Socho just cited. One wonders whether, after all, justice is done to the Hindus. One sees how easily Jewish teaching can be distorted into a doctrine of calculated Zechuth. Are the Hindus being misjudged equally? Certainly, in some cases this must be so, for Professor Oman, with his remarkably sympathetic insight, records experiences such as this more than once (p. 147). He is describing one of the Jain ascetics, and remarks:

"His personal appearance gave the impression of great suffering, and his attendants all had the same appearance, contrasting very much indeed with the ordinary Sadhus of other sects. And wherefore this austere rejection of the world's goods, wherefore all this self-inflicted misery? Is it to attain a glorious Heaven hereafter, a blessed existence after death? No! It is, as the old monk explained to me, only to escape rebirth–for the Jain believes in the transmigration of souls–and to attain rest."

Other ascetics gave similar explanations. Thus (p. 100):

"The Christian missionary entered into conversation with the Hermit (a Bairagi from the Upper Provinces), and learned from him that he had adopted a life of abstraction and isolation from the world, neither to expiate any sin, nor to secure any reward. He averred that he had no desires and no hopes, but that, being removed from the agitations of the worldly life, he was full of tranquil joy."

VI. Lost Purim Joys

It is scarcely accurate to assert, as is sometimes done, that the most characteristic of the Purim pranks of the past were children of the Ghetto, and came to a natural end when the Ghetto walls fell. In point of fact, most of these joys originated before the era of the Ghetto, and others were introduced for the first time when Ghetto life was about to fade away into history.

Probably the oldest of Purim pranks was the bonfire and the burning of an effigy. Now, so far from being a Ghetto custom, it did not even emanate from Europe, the continent of Ghettos; it belongs to Babylonia and Persia. This is what was done, according to an old Geonic account recovered by Professor L. Ginzberg:

"It is customary in Babylonia and Elam for boys to make an effigy resembling Haman; this they suspend on their roofs, four or five days before Purim. On Purim day they erect a bonfire, and cast the effigy into its midst, while the boys stand round about it, jesting and singing. And they have a ring suspended in the midst of the fire, which (ring) they hold and wave from one side of the fire to the other."

Bonfires, it may be thought, need no recondite explanation; light goes with a light heart, and boys always love a blaze. Dr. J.G. Frazer, in his "Golden Bough," has endeavored, nevertheless, to bring the Purim bonfire into relation with primitive spring-tide and midsummer conflagrations, which survived into modern carnivals, but did not originate with them. Such bonfires belonged to what has been called sympathetic or homeopathic magic; by raising an artificial heat, you ensured a plentiful dose of the natural heat of the sun. So, too, the burning of an effigy was not, in the first instance, a malicious or unfriendly act. A tree-spirit, or a figure representing the spirit of vegetation, was consumed in fire, but the spirit was regarded as beneficent, not hostile, and by burning a friendly deity the succor of the sun was gained. Dr. Frazer cites some evidence for the early prevalence of the Purim bonfire; he argues strongly and persuasively in favor of the identification of Purim with the Babylonian feast of the Sacaea, a wild, extravagant bacchanalian revel, which, in the old Asiatic world, much resembled the Saturnalia of a later Italy. The theory is plausible, though it is not quite proven by Dr. Frazer, but it seems to me that whatever be the case with Purim generally, there is one hitherto overlooked feature of the Purim bonfire that does clearly connect it with the other primitive conflagrations of which mention was made above.

This overlooked feature is the "ring." No explanation is given by the Gaon as to its purpose in the tenth century, and it can hardly have been used to hold the effigy. Now, in many of the primitive bonfires, the fire was produced by aid of a revolving wheel. This wheel typifies the sun. Waving the "ring" in the Purim bonfires has obviously the same significance, and this apparently inexplicable feature does, I think, serve to link the ancient Purim prank with a long series of old-world customs, which, it need hardly be said, have nothing whatever to do with the Ghetto.

Then, again, the most famous of Purim parodies preceded the Ghetto period. The official Ghetto begins with the opening of the sixteenth century, whereas the best parodies belong to a much earlier date, the fourteenth century. Such parodies, in which sacred things are the subject of harmless jest, are purely medieval in spirit, as well as in date. Exaggerated praises of wine were a foil to the sobriety of the Jew, the fun consisting in this conscious exaggeration. The medieval Jew, be it remembered, drew no severe line between sacred and profane. All life was to him equally holy, equally secular. So it is not strange that we find included in sacred Hebrew hymnologies wine-songs for Purim and Chanukah and other Synagogue feasts, and these songs are at least as old as the early part of the twelfth century. For Purim, many Synagogue liturgies contain serious additions for each of the eighteen benedictions of the Amidah prayer, and equally serious paraphrases of Esther, some of them in Aramaic, abound among the Genizah fragments in Cambridge. Besides these, however, are many harmlessly humorous jingles and rhymes which were sung in the synagogue, admittedly for the amusement of the children, and for the child-hearts of adult growth. For them, too, the Midrash had played round Haman, reviling him, poking fun at him, covering him with ridicule rather than execration. It is true that the earliest ritual reference to the wearing of masks on Purim dates from the year 1508, just within the Ghetto period. But this omission of earlier reference is surely an accident, In the Babylonian Sacaea, cited above, a feature of the revel was that men and women disguised themselves, a slave dressed up as king, while servants personated masters, and vice versa. All these elements of carnival exhilaration are much earlier than the Middle Ages. Ghetto days, however, originated, perhaps, the stamping of feet, clapping of hands, clashing of mallets, and smashing of earthenware pots, to punctuate certain passages of the Esther story and of the subsequent benediction.

My strongest point concerns what, beyond all other delights, has been regarded as the characteristic amusement of the festival, viz. the Purim play. We not only possess absolutely no evidence that Purim plays were performed in the Ghettos till the beginning of the eighteenth century, when the end of the Ghettos was almost within sight, but the extant references imply that they were then a novelty. Plays on the subject of Esther were very common in medieval Europe during earlier centuries, but these plays were written by Christians, not by Jews, and were performed by monks, not by Rabbis. Strange as it may seem, it is none the less the fact that the Purim play belongs to the most recent of the Purim amusements, and that its life has been short and, on the whole, inglorious.

Thus, without pressing the contention too closely, Purim festivities do not deserve to be tarred with the Ghetto brush. Is it, then, denied that Purim was more mirthfully observed in Ghetto days than it is at the present day? By no means. It is unquestionable that Purim used to be a merrier anniversary than it is now. The explanation is simple. In part, the change has arisen through a laudable disinclination from pranks that may be misconstrued as tokens of vindictiveness against an ancient foe or his modern reincarnations. As a second cause may be assigned the growing and regrettable propensity of Jews to draw a rigid line of separation between life and religion, and wherever this occurs, religious feasts tend towards a solemnity that cannot, and dare not, relax into amusement. This tendency is eating at the very heart of Jewish life, and ought to be resisted by all who truly understand the genius of Judaism.

But the psychology of the change goes even deeper. The Jew is emotional, but he detests making a display of his feelings to mere onlookers. The Wailing Wall scenes at Jerusalem are not a real exception–the facts are "Cooked," to meet the demands of clamant tourists. The Jew's sensitiveness is the correlative of his emotionalism. While all present are joining in the game, each Jew will play with full abandonment to the humor of the moment. But as soon as some play the part of spectators, the Jew feels his limbs growing too stiff for dancing, his voice too hushed for song. All must participate, or all must leave off. Thus, a crowd of Italians or Southern French may play at carnival to-day to amuse sight-seers in the Riviera, but Jews have never consented, have never been able, to sport that others might stand by and laugh at, and not with, the sportsmen. In short, Purim has lost its character, because Jews have lost their character, their disposition for innocent, unanimous joyousness. We are no longer so closely united in interests or in local abodes that we could, on the one hand, enjoy ourselves as one man, and, on the other, play merry pranks, without incurring the criticism of indifferent, cold-eyed observers. Criticism has attacked the authenticity of the Esther story, and proposed Marduk for Mordecai, and Istar for Esther. But criticism of another kind has worked far more havoc, for its "superior" airs have killed the Purim joy. Perhaps it is not quite dead after all.

VII. Jews and Letters

The jubilee of the introduction of the Penny Post into England was not reached till 1890. It is difficult to realize the state of affairs before this reform became part of our everyday life. That less than three-quarters of a century ago the scattered members of English families were, in a multitude of cases, practically dead to one another, may incline one to exaggerate the insignificance of the means of communication in times yet more remote. Certainly, in ancient Judea there were fewer needs than in the modern world. Necessity produces invention, and as the Jew of remote times rarely felt a strong necessity to correspond with his brethren in his own or other countries, it naturally followed that the means of communication were equally extempore in character. It may be of interest to put together some desultory jottings on this important topic.

The way to Judea lies through Rome. If we wish information whether the Jews knew anything of a regular post, we must first inquire whether the Romans possessed that institution. According to Gibbon, this was the case. Excellent roads made their appearance wherever the Romans settled; and "the advantage of receiving the earliest intelligence and of conveying their orders with celerity, induced the Emperors to establish throughout their extensive dominions the regular institution of posts. Houses were everywhere erected at the distance only of five or six miles; each of them was constantly provided with forty horses, and by the help of these relays it was easy to travel a hundred miles a day along the Roman roads. The use of the posts was allowed to those who claimed it by an Imperial mandate; but, though originally intended for the public service, it was sometimes indulged to the business or con-veniency of private citizens." This statement of Gibbon (towards the end of chapter ii) applies chiefly, then, to official despatches; for we know from other sources that the Romans had no public post as we understand the term, but used special messengers (tabellarius) to convey private letters.

Exactly the same facts meet us with reference to the Jews in the earlier Talmudic times. There were special Jewish letter-carriers, who carried the documents in a pocket made for the purpose, and in several towns in Palestine there was a kind of regular postal arrangement, though many places were devoid of the institution. It is impossible to suppose that these postal conveniences refer only to official documents; for the Mishnah (Sabbath, x, 4) is evidently speaking of Jewish postmen, who, at that time, would hardly have been employed to carry the despatches of the government. The Jewish name for this post was Bê-Davvar, and apparently was a permanent and regular institution. From a remark of Rabbi Jehudah (Rosh ha-Shanah, 9b), "like a postman who goes about everywhere and carries merchandise to the whole province," it would seem that the Jews had established a parcels-post; but unfortunately we have no precise information as to how these posts were managed.

Gibbon's account of the Roman post recalls another Jewish institution, which may have been somehow connected with the Bê-Davvar. The official custodian of the goat that was sent into the wilderness on the Day of Atonement was allowed, if he should feel the necessity–a necessity which, according to tradition, never arose–to partake of food even on the fast-day. For this purpose huts were erected along the route, and men provided with food were stationed at each of these huts to meet the messenger and conduct him some distance on his way.

That the postal system cannot have been very much developed, is clear from the means adopted to announce the New Moon in various localities. This official announcement certainly necessitated a complete system of communication. At first, we are told (Rosh ha-Shanah, ii, 2), fires were lighted on the tops of the mountains; but the Samaritans seem to have ignited the beacons at the wrong time, so as to deceive the Jews. It was, therefore, decided to communicate the news by messenger. The mountain-fires were prepared as follows: Long staves of cedar-wood, canes, and branches of the olive-tree were tied up with coarse threads or flax; these were lighted as torches, and men on the hills waved the brands to and fro, upward and downward, until the signal was repeated on the next hill, and so forth. When messengers were substituted for these fire signals, it does not appear that they carried letters; they brought verbal messages, which they seem to have shouted out without necessarily dismounting from the animals they rode. Messages were not sent every month, but only six times a year; and a curious light is thrown on the means of communication of the time, by the legal decision that anyone was to be believed on the subject, and that the word of a passing merchant who said that "he had heard the New Moon proclaimed," was to be accepted unhesitatingly. Nowadays, busy men are sometimes put out by postal vagaries, but they hardly suffer to the extent of having to fast two days. This calamity is recorded, however, in the Jerusalem Talmud, as having, on a certain occasion, resulted from the delay in the arrival of the messengers announcing the New Moon.

Besides the proclamation of the New Moon, other official documents must have been despatched regularly. "Bills of divorce," for instance, needed special messengers; the whole question of the legal position of messengers is very intimately bound up with that of conveying divorces. This, however, seems to have been the function of private messengers, who were not in the strict sense letter-carriers at all. It may be well, in passing, to recall one or two other means of communication mentioned in the Midrash. Thus we read how Joshua, with twelve thousand of his warriors, was imprisoned, by means of witchcraft, within a sevenfold barrier of iron. He resolves to write for aid to the chief of the tribe of Reuben, bidding him to summon Phineas, who is to bring the "trumpets" with him. Joshua ties the message to the wings of a dove, or pigeon, and the bird carries the letter to the Israelites, who speedily arrive with Phineas and the trumpets, and, after routing the enemy, effect Joshua's rescue. A similar idea may be found in the commentary of Kimchi on Genesis. Noah, wishing for information, says Kimchi, sent forth a raven, but it brought back no message; then he sent a dove, which has a natural capacity for bringing back replies, when it has been on the same way once or twice. Thus kings train these birds for the purpose of sending them great distances, with letters tied to their wings. So we read (Sabbath, 49) in the Talmud that "a dove's wings protect it," i.e. people preserve it, and do not slay it, because they train it to act as their messenger. Or, again, we find arrows used as a means of carrying letters, and we are not alluding to such signals as Jonathan gave to David. During the siege of Jerusalem by the Romans, the Emperor had men placed near the walls of Jerusalem, and they wrote the information they obtained on arrows, and fired them from the wall, with the connivance, probably, of the philo-Roman party that existed within the doomed city.

In earlier Bible times, there was, as the Tell-el-Amarna bricks show, an extensive official correspondence between Canaan and Egypt, but private letter-writing seems not to have been resorted to; messages were transmitted orally to the parties concerned. This fact is well illustrated by the story of Joseph. He may, of course, have deliberately resolved not to communicate with his family, but if letter-writing had been usual, his brothers would naturally have asked him–a question that did not suggest itself to them–why he had never written to tell his father of his fortunes. When Saul desired to summon Israel, he sent, not a letter, but a mutilated yoke of oxen; the earliest letter mentioned in the Bible being that in which King David ordered Uriah to be placed in the forefront of the army. Jezebel sends letters in Ahab's name to Naboth, Jehu to Samaria. In all these cases letters were used for treacherous purposes, and they are all short. Probably the authors of these plots feared to betray their real intention orally, and so they committed their orders to writing, expecting their correspondents to read between the lines. It is not till the time of Isaiah that the references to writing become frequent. Intercourse between Palestine on the one hand and Babylon and Egypt on the other had then increased greatly, and the severance of the nation itself tended to make correspondence through writing more necessary. When we reach the age of Jeremiah, this fact makes itself even more strongly apparent. Letters are often mentioned by that prophet (xxix. 25, 29), and a professional class of Soferim, or scribes, make their appearance. Afterwards, of course, the Sofer became of much higher importance; he was not merely a professional writer, but a man learned in the Law, who spread the knowledge of it among the people. Later, again, these functions were separated, and the Sofer added to his other offices that of teacher of the young. Nowadays, he has regained his earlier and less important position, for the modern Sofer is simply a professional writer. In the time of Ezekiel (ix. 2) the Sofer went abroad with the implements of his trade, including the inkhorn, at his side. In the Talmud, the scribe is sometimes described by his Latin title libellarius (Sabbath,11a). The Jews of Egypt, as may be seen from the Assouan Papyri, wrote home in cases of need in the time of Nehemiah; and in the same age we hear also of "open letters," for Sanballat sends a missive of that description by his servant; and apparently it was by means of a similar letter that the festival of Purim was announced to the Jews (Esther ix., where, unlike the other passages quoted, the exact words of the letter of Mordecai are not given). The order to celebrate Chanukah was published in the same way, and, indeed, the books of the Apocrypha contain many interesting letters, and in the pages of Josephus the Jews hold frequent intercourse in this way with many foreign countries. In the latter cases, when the respective kings corresponded, the letters were conveyed by special embassies.

  One might expect this epistolary activity to display itself at an even more developed stage in the records of Rabbinical times. But this is by no means the case, for the Rabbinical references to letters in the beginning of the common era are few and far between. Polemic epistles make their appearance; but they are the letters of non-Jewish missionaries like Paul. This form of polemical writing possessed many advantages; the letters were passed on from one reader to another; they would be read aloud, too, before gatherings of the people to whom they were addressed. Maimonides, in later times, frequently adopted this method of communicating with whole communities, and many of the Geonim and other Jewish authorities followed the same plan. But somehow the device seems not to have commended itself to the earliest Rabbis. Though we read of many personal visits paid by the respective authorities of Babylon and Palestine to one another, yet they appear to have corresponded very rarely in writing. The reason lay probably in the objection felt against committing the Halachic, or legal, decisions of the schools to writing, and there was little else of consequence to communicate after the failure of Bar-Cochba's revolt against the Roman rule.

It must not be thought, however, that this prohibition had the effect we have described for very long. Rabbi Gamaliel, Rabbi Chananiah, and many others had frequent correspondence with far distant places, and as soon as the Mishnah acquired a fixed form, even though it was not immediately committed to writing, the recourse to letters became much more common. Pupils of the compilers of the Mishnah proceeded to Babylon to spread its influence, and they naturally maintained a correspondence with their chiefs in Palestine. Rab and Samuel in particular, among the Amoraim, were regular letter-writers, and Rabbi Jochanan replied to them. Towards the end of the third century this correspondence between Judea and Babylon became even more active. Abitur and Abin often wrote concerning legal decisions and the doings of the schools, and thereby the intellectual activity of Judaism maintained its solidarity despite the fact that the Jewish people was no longer united in one land. In the Talmud we frequently read, "they sent from there," viz. Palestine. Obviously these messages were sent in writing, though possibly the bearer of the message was often himself a scholar, who conveyed his report by word of mouth. Perhaps the growth of the Rabbi's practice of writing responses to questions–a practice that became so markedly popular in subsequent centuries–may be connected with the similar habit of the Roman jurists and the Christian Church fathers, and the form of response adopted by the eighth century Geonim is reminiscent of that of the Roman lawyers. The substance of the letters, however, is by no means the same; the Church father wrote on dogmatic, the Rabbi on legal, questions. Between the middle of the fourth century and the time of the Geonim, we find no information as to the use of letters among the Jews. From that period onwards, however, Jews became very diligent letter-writers, and sometimes, for instance in the case of the "Guide of the Perplexed" of Maimonides, whole works were transmitted in the form of letters. The scattering of Israel, too, rendered it important to Jews to obtain information of the fortunes of their brethren in different parts of the world. Rumors of Messianic appearances from the twelfth century onwards, the contest with regard to the study of philosophy, the fame of individual Rabbis, the rise of a class of travellers who made very long and dangerous journeys, all tended to increase the facilities and necessities of intercourse by letter. It was long, however, before correspondence became easy or safe. Not everyone is possessed of the postmen assigned in Midrashim to King Solomon, who pressed demons into his service, and forced them to carry his letters wheresoever he willed. Chasdai experienced considerable difficulty in transmitting his famous letter to the king of the Chazars, and that despite his position of authority in the Spanish State. In 960 a letter on some question of Kasher was sent from the Rhine to Palestine–proof of the way in which the most remote Jewish communities corresponded.

    The question of the materials used in writing has an important bearing on our subject. Of course, the ritual regulations for writing the holy books, the special preparation of the parchment, the ink, the strict rules for the formation of the letters, hardly fall within the province of this article. In ancient times the most diverse substances were used for writing on. Palm-leaves (for which Palestine of old was famous) were a common object for the purpose, being so used all over Asia. Some authorities believe that in the time of Moses the palm leaf was the ordinary writing-material. Olive-leaves, again, were thick and hard, while carob-leaves (St. John's bread), besides being smooth, long, and broad, were evergreen, and thus eminently fitted for writing. Walnut shells, pomegranate skins, leaves of gourds, onion-leaves, lettuce-heads, even the horns of cattle, and the human body, letters being tattooed on the hands of slaves, were all turned to account. It is maintained by some that leather was the original writing-material of the Hebrews; others, again, give their vote in favor of linen, though the Talmud does not mention the latter material in connection with writing. Some time after Alexander the Great, the

Egyptian papyrus became common in Palestine, where it probably was known earlier, as Jewish letters on papyrus were sent to Jerusalem from the Fayyum in the fifth century B.C.E. Even as late as Maimonides, the scrolls of the Law were written on leather, and not on parchment, which is now the ordinary material for the purpose. That the Torah was not to be written on a vegetable product was an assumed first principle. The Samaritans went so far as to insist that the animal whose hide was needed for so holy a purpose, must be slain Kasher. Similarly with divorce documents. A Get on paper would be held legal post factum, though it is not allowed to use that material, as it is easily destroyed or mutilated, and the use of paper for the purpose was confined to the East. Some allowed the Book of Esther to be read from a paper copy; other authorities not only strongly objected to this, but even forbade the reading of the Haftarah from paper. Hence one finds in libraries so many parchment scrolls containing only the Haftarahs. The Hebrew word for letter, Iggereth, is of unknown origin, though it is now commonly taken to be an Assyrian loan-word. It used to be derived from a root signifying to "hire," in reference to the "hired courier," by whom it was despatched. Other terms for letter, such as "book," "roll," explain themselves. Black ink was early used, though it is certain that it was either kept in a solid state, like India ink, or that it was of the consistency of glue, and needed the application of water before it could be used. For pens, the iron stylus, the reed, needle, and quill (though the last was not admitted without a struggle) were the common substitutes at various dates.

We must now return to the subject with which we set out, and make a few supplementary remarks with regard to the actual conveyance of letters. In the Talmud (Baba Mezia, 83b) a proverb is quoted to this effect, "He who can read and understand the contents of a letter, may be the deliverer thereof." As a rule, one would prefer that the postman did not read the correspondence he carries, and this difficulty seems to have stood in the way of trusting letters to unknown bearers. To remove this obstacle to free intercourse, Rabbenu Gershom issued his well-known decree, under penalty of excommunication, against anyone who, entrusted with a letter to another, made himself master of its contents. To the present day, in some places, the Jewish writer writes on the outside of his letter, the abbreviation [Hebrew:

beth-cheth-daleth-resh-"-gimel], which alludes to this injunction of Rabbenu Gershom. Again, the Sabbath was and still is a difficulty with observant Jews. Rabbi Jose ha-Cohen is mentioned in the Talmud (Sabbath, 19a) as deserving of the following compliment. He never allowed a letter of his to get into the hands of a non-Jew, for fear he might carry it on the Sabbath, and strict laws are laid down on the subject. That Christians in modern times entrusted their letters to Jews goes without saying, and even in places where this is not commonly allowed, the non-Jew is employed when the letter contains bad news. Perhaps for this reason Rabbenu Jacob Tarn permitted divorces to be sent by post, though the controversy on the legality of such delivery is, I believe, still undecided.

Besides packmen, who would often be the medium by which letters were transmitted, there was in some Jewish communities a special class that devoted themselves to a particular branch of the profession. They made it their business to seek out lost sons and deliver messages to them from their anxious parents. Some later Jewish authorities, in view of the distress that the silence of absent loved ones causes to those at home, lay down the rule that the duty of honoring parents, the fifth commandment, includes the task of corresponding when absent from them. These peripatetic letter-carriers also conveyed the documents of divorce to women that would otherwise be in the unpleasant condition of being neither married nor single. Among the most regular and punctual of Jewish postmen may be mentioned the bearers of begging letters and begging books. There is no fear that these will not be duly delivered.

Our reference to letters of recommendation reminds us of an act, on the part of a modern Rabbi, of supererogation in the path of honesty. The post is in the hands of the Government, and, accordingly, the late Rabbi Bamberger of Wurzburg, whenever he gave a Haskamah, or recommendation, which would be delivered by hand, was wont to destroy a postage stamp, so as not to defraud the Government, even in appearance. With this remarkable instance of conscientious uprightness, we may fitly conclude this notice, suggested as it has been by the modern improvements in the postal system, which depend for their success so largely on the honesty of the public.

VIII. The Shape of Matzoth

Dr. Johnson said, "It is easier to know that a cake is bad than to make a good one." I had a tiny quantity of material which, by dint of much rolling, I might have expanded into a broad, flat, unsubstantial whole; I preferred, however, to make of my little piece of dough a little cake, small and therefore less pretentious. I am afraid that even in this concentrated form it will prove flavorless and indigestible, but the cook must be blamed, not the material.

I have no intention to consider the various operations connected with the preparation of unleavened Passover cakes: the kneading, the ingredients, the curious regulations regarding the water used, such precautions as carefully watching the ovens. Those who are inclined to connect some of these customs with the practices of non-Jewish peoples will find some interesting facts on all theses topics; but what I wish to speak of now is the shape and form of Passover cakes.

The Christian emblems that figure in the celebration of the Eucharist, or Lord's Supper, were probably derived from the ceremonies of the Passover eve. The bread employed in the Eucharist is with some Christian sects unleavened, and, indeed, leavened cakes seem to have been introduced solely as a protest against certain so-called Judaizing tendencies. The Latin Church still contends for the propriety of employing unleavened bread, and from the seventh century unleavened bread was used at Rome and leavened bread at Constantinople. From the earliest times, however, the Eucharistic loaves were invariably round in shape, there being, indeed, a supposed edict by Pope Zephyrinus (197-217) to that effect. It is passing strange that Bona, an ecclesiastical writer, derived this roundness from the shape of the coins Judas received for betraying his master. But though there is no distinct enactment either in the Talmud or in any of the later codes as to what the form of the Matzoth must be, these have been from time immemorial round also. Some Minhagim are more firmly rooted than actual laws, and this custom is one of them. In one of his cartoons, Picard has an illustration which is apparently that of a squarish Matzah; this may, however, be only a case of defective drawing. It is true that in Roumania square Matzoth are used, but in the controversy raised by the introduction of Matzah-making machines, the opponents of the change argued as though no other than a round shape were conceivable. Kluger, for instance, never seems to have realized that his weightiest objection to the use of the machine would be obviated by making the Matzoth square or rectangular. When it was first proposed to introduce Matzah machines in London, the resistance came chiefly from the manufacturers, and not from the ecclesiastical authorities. The bakers refused categorically to make square Matzoth, declaring that if they did so, their stock would be unsalable. Even to the present day no square Matzoth are baked in London; those occasionally seen there are imported from the Continent. The ancient Egyptians made their cakes round, and the Matzoth are regarded Midrashically as a memorial of the food which the Egyptian masters forced on their Israelite slaves. A round shape is apparently the simplest symmetrical form, but beyond this I fancy that the round form of the Passover bread is partly due to the double meaning of Uggoth Matzoth. The word Uggoth signifies cakes baked in the sand or hot embers; but Uggah also means a "circle." To return, however, to the Eucharistic wafers.

A further point of identity, though only a minute detail, can be traced in the regulation that the Eucharistic oblate from which the priest communicated was, in the ninth century, larger than the loaves used by the people. So the Passover cakes (Shimmurim) used by the master of the house, and particularly the middle cake, pieces of which were distributed, were made larger than the ordinary Matzoth. Picard (1723) curiously enough reverses this relation, and draws the ordinary Matzoth much larger and thicker than the Shimmurim. The ordinary Matzoth he represents as thick oval cakes, with a single coil of large holes, which start outwards from the centre. Picard speaks of Matzoth made in different shapes, but he gives no details.

In the Middle Ages, and, indeed, as early as Chrysostom (fourth century), the Church cakes were marked with a cross, and bore various inscriptions. In the Coptic Church, for example, the legend was "Holy! holy! holy is the Lord of hosts." Now, in a Latin work, Roma subterranea, about 1650, a statement is made which seems to imply that the Passover cakes of the Jews were also marked with crosses. What can have led to this notion? The origin is simple enough. The ancient Romans, as Aringhus himself writes, and as Virgil, Horace, and Martial frequently mention, made their loaves with cross indentations, in order to facilitate dividing them into four parts: much as nowadays Scotch scones are baked four together, and the central dividing lines give the fourfold scone the appearance of bearing a cross mark. It may be that the Jews made their Passover cakes, which were thicker than ours and harder to break, in the same way. But, besides, the small holes and indentations that cover the surface of the modern Matzah might, if the Matzah be held in certain positions, possibly be mistaken for a cross. These indentations are, I should add, very ancient, being referred to in the Talmud, and, if I may venture a suggestion, also in the Bible, I Kings xiv. 3, and elsewhere, Nekudim being cakes punctuated with small interstices.

We can carry the explanation a little further. The three Matzoth Shimmurim used in the Haggadah Service were made with especial care, and in medieval times were denominated Priest, Levite, Israelite, in order to discriminate among them. Picard, by an amusing blunder, speaks of a gateau des lévites; he, of course, means the middle cake. From several authorities it is clear that the three Matzoth were inscribed in some cases with these three words, in others with the letters Alef, Beth, Gimmel, in order to distinguish them. A rough Alef would not look unlike a cross. Later on, the three Matzoth were distinguished by one, two, three indentations respectively, as in the Roman numerals; and even at the present day care is sometimes taken, though in other ways, to prevent the Priest, Levite, and Israelite from falling into confusion. I do not know whether the stringent prohibition, by the Shulchan Aruch, of "shaped or marked cakes" for use on Passover, may not be due to the fact that the Eucharistic cakes used by Christians were marked with letters and symbols. Certain it is that the prohibition of these "shaped" cakes is rather less emphatic in the Talmud than in the later authorities, who up to a certain date are never weary of condemning or at least discouraging the practice. The custom of using these cakes is proved to be widespread by the very frequency of the prohibitions, and they were certainly common in the beginning of the sixteenth century, from which period seems to date the custom of making the Matzoth very thin, though the thicker species has not been entirely superseded even up to the present day. In the East the Matzoth are still made very thick and unpalatable. They cannot be eaten as they are; they are either softened, by being dipped in some liquid, or they are ground down to meal, and then remade into smaller and more edible cakes.

The Talmud mentions a "stamp" in connection with "shaped cakes," which Buxtorf takes for Lebkuchen, and Levy for scalloped and fancifully-edged cakes. The Geonim, however, explain that they were made in the forms of birds, beasts, and fishes. I have seen Matzoth made in this way in London, and have myself eaten many a Matzah sheep and monkey, but, unfortunately, I cannot recollect whether it was during Passover. In Holland, these shaped cakes are still used, but in "strict" families only before the Passover.

Limits of space will not allow me to quote some interesting notes with reference to Hebrew inscriptions on cakes generally, which would furnish parallels to the Holy! holy! of the Coptic wafers. Children received such cakes as a "specific for becoming wise." Some directions may be found in Sefer Raziel for making charm-cakes, which must have been the reverse of charming from the unutterable names of angels written on them. One such charm, however, published by Horwitz, I cannot refrain from mentioning, as it is very curious and practical. It constitutes a never-failing antidote to forgetfulness, and, for aught I know, may be quite as efficacious as some of the quack mnemonic systems extensively advertised nowadays.

"The following hath been tried and found reliable, and Rabbi Saadia ben Joseph made use of it. He discovered it in the cave of Rabbi Eleazar Kalir, and all the wise men of Israel together with their pupils applied the remedy with excellent effect:–At the beginning of the month of Sivan take some wheatmeal and knead it, and be sure to remain standing. Make cakes and bake them, write thereon the verse, 'Memory hath He made among His wondrous acts: gracious and merciful is the Lord.' Take an egg and boil it hard, peel it, and write on it the names of five angels; eat such a cake every day, for thirty days, with an egg, and thou wilt learn all thou seest, and wilt never forget."

The manuscript illuminated Haggadahs are replete with interest and information. But I must avoid further observations on these manuscripts except in so far as they illustrate my present subject. In the Haggadah the question is asked, "Why do we eat this Matzah?" and at the words "this Matzah" the illuminated manuscripts contain, in the great majority of cases, representations of Matzoth. These in some instances present rather interesting features, which may throw historical light on the archeology of the subject. Some of these figured Matzoth are oval, one I have seen star-shaped, but almost all are circular in form. Many, however, unlike the modern Matzah and owing to the shape of the mould, have a broad border distinct from the rest of the cake. The Crawford Haggadah, now in the Ryland library, Manchester, pictures a round Matzah through which a pretty flowered design runs. Others, again, and this I think a very ancient, as it certainly is a very common, design, are covered with transverse lines, which result in producing diamond-shaped spaces with a very pleasing effect, resembling somewhat the appearance of the lattice work cakes used in Italy and Persia, I think. The lines, unless they be mere pictorial embellishments, are, possibly, as in the Leeds cakes, rows of indentations resulting from the punctuation of the Matzah. In one British Museum manuscript (Roman rite, 1482), the star and diamond shapes are combined, the border being surrounded with small triangles, and the centre of the cake being divided into diamond-like sections. In yet another manuscript the Matzah has a border, divided by small lines into almost rectangular sections, while the body of the cake is ornamented with a design in which variously shaped figures, quadrilaterals and triangles, are irregularly interspersed. One fanciful picture deserves special mention, as it is the only one of the kind in all the illustrated manuscripts and printed Haggadahs in the Oxford and British Museum libraries. This Matzah occurs in an Italian manuscript of the fourteenth century. It is adorned with a flowered border, and in the centre appears a human-faced quadruped of apparently Egyptian character.

    Poetry and imagination are displayed in some of these devices, but in only one or two cases did the artists attain high levels of picturesque illustration. How suggestive, for instance, is the chain pattern, adopted in a manuscript of the Michaelis Collection at Oxford. It must not be thought that this idea at least was never literally realized, for only last year I was shown a Matzah made after a very similar design, possibly not for use on the first two nights of Passover. The bread of affliction recalls the Egyptian bonds, and it is an ingenious idea to bid us ourselves turn the ancient chains to profitable use–by eating them. This expressive design is surpassed by another, found in a beautifully-illuminated manuscript of the fourteenth century. This Matzah bears a curious device in the centre: it is a prison door modelled with considerable skill, but I do not suppose that Matzoth were ever made in this fashion.

Notes

"The Book of Delight"

The connection between Zabara's work and the Solomon and Marcolf legend was first pointed out in my "Short History of Jewish Literature" (1906), p. 95. I had long before detected the resemblance, though I was not aware of it when I wrote an essay on Zabara in the Jewish Quarterly Review. To the latter (vi, pp. 502 et seq.) the reader is referred for bibliographical notes, and also for details on the textual relations of the two editions of Zabara's poem.

A number of parallels with other folk-literatures are there indicated; others have been added by Dr. Israel Davidson, in his edition of the "Three Satires" (New York, 1904), which accompany the "Book of Delight" in the Constantinople edition, and are also possibly by Zabara.

The late Professor David Kaufmann informed me some years ago that he had a manuscript of the poem in his possession. But, after his death, the manuscript could not be found in his library. Should it eventually be rediscovered, it would be desirable to have a new, carefully printed edition of the Hebrew text of the "Book of Delight." I would gladly place at the disposal of the editor my copy of the Constantinople edition, made from the Oxford specimen. The Bodleian copy does not seem to be unique, as had been supposed.

The literature on the Solomon and Marcolf legend is extensive. The following references may suffice. J.M. Kemble published (London, 1848) "The Dialogue of Solomon and Saturnus," for the Aelfric Society. "Of all the forms of the story yet preserved," says Mr. Kemble, "the Anglo-Saxon are undoubtedly the oldest." He talks vaguely of the intermixture of Oriental elements, but assigns a northern origin to one portion of the story. Crimm had argued for a Hebrew souice, thinking Marcolf a name of scorn in Hebrew. But the Hebrew Marcolis (or however one may spell it) is simply Mercury. In the Latin version, however, Marcolf is distinctly represented as coming from the East. William of Tyre (12th cent.) suggests the identity of Marcolf with Abdemon, whom Josephus ("Antiquities," VIII, v, 3) names as Hiram's Riddle-

Guesser. A useful English edition is E. Gordon Duff's "Dialogue or Communing between the Wise King Salomon and Marcolphus" (London, 1892). Here, too, as in the Latin version, Marcolf is a man from the Orient. Besides these books, two German works deserve special mention. F. Vogt, in his essay entitled Die deutschen Dichtungen won Salomon und Markolf, which appeared in Halle, in 1880, also thinks Marcolf an Eastern. Finally, as the second part of his "Untersuchungen zur mittelhochdeutschen Spielmannspoesie" (Schwerin, 1894), H. Tardel published Zum Salman-Morolf. Tardel is skeptical as to the Eastern provenance of the legend.

It has been thought that a form of this legend is referred to in the fifth century. The Contradictio Solomonis, which Pope Gelasius excluded from the sacred canon, has been identified with some version of the Marcolf story.

A Visit to Hebron

The account of Hebron, given in this volume, must be read for what it was designed to be, an impressionist sketch. The history of the site, in so far as it has been written, must be sought in more technical books. As will be seen from several details, my visit was paid in the month of April, just before Passover. Things have altered in some particulars since I was there, but there has been no essential change in the past decade.

The Hebron Haram, or shrine over the Cave of Machpelah, is fully described in the "Cruise of H.M.S. Bacchante, 1879-1882," ii, pp. 595-619. (Compare "Survey of Western Palestine," iii, pp. 333-346; and the Quarterly Statement of the Palestine Exploration Fund, 1882, pp. 197-214.) Colonel Conder's account narrates the experiences of the present King of England at the Haram in April, 1882. Dean Stanley had previously entered the Haram with King Edward VII, in January, 1862 (see Stanley's "Sermons in the East," 1863, pp. 141-169). A good note on the relation between these modern narratives and David Reubeni's (dating from the early part of the sixteenth century) was contributed by Canon Dalton to the Quarterly Statement, 1897, p. 53. A capital plan of the Haram is there printed.

Mr. Adler's account of his visit to Hebron will be found in his "Jews in Many Lands," pp. 104-111; he tells of his entry into the Haram on pp. 137-138.

M. Lucien Gautier's work referred to is his Souvenirs du Terre-Sainte (Lausanne, 1898). The description of glass-making appears on p. 53 of that work.

The somewhat startling identification of the Ramet el-Khalil, near Hebron, with the site of the altar built by Samuel in Ramah (I Sam. vii. 17) is justified at length in Mr. Shaw Caldecott's book "The Tabernacle, its History and Structure" (London, 1904).

The Solace of Books (pp. 93-121)

The opening quotation is from the Ethical Will of Judah ibn Tibbon, the "father" of Jewish translators. The original is fully analyzed in an essay by the present writer, in the Jewish Quarterly Review, iii, 453. See also ibidem, p. 483. The Hebrew text was printed by Edelmann, and also by Steinschneider; by the latter at Berlin, 1852.

A writer much cited in this same essay, Richard of Bury, derived his name from his birthplace, Bury St. Edmunds. "He tells us himself in his 'Philobiblon' that he used his high offices of state as a means of collecting books. He let it be known that books were the most acceptable presents that could be made to him" ("Dictionary of National Biography," viii, 26). He was also a student of Hebrew, and collected grammars of that language. Altogether his "Philobiblon" is an "admirable exhibition of the temper of a book-lover." Written in the early part of the fourteenth century, the "Philobiblon" was first published, at Cologne, in 1473. The English edition cited in this essay is that published in the King's Classics (De la More Library, ed. I. Gollancz).

The citation from Montaigne is from his essay on the "Three Commerces" (bk. in, ch. iii). The same passages, in Florio's rendering, will be found in Mr. A.R. Waller's edition (Dent's Everyman's Library), in, pp. 48-50. Of the three "Commerces" (i.e. societies)–Men, Women, and Books–Montaigne proclaims that the commerce of books "is much more solid-sure and much more ours." I have claimed Montaigne as the great-grandson of a Spanish Jew on the authority of Mr. Waller (Introduction, p. vii).

The paragraphs on books from the "Book of the Pious," §§ 873-932, have been collected (and translated into English) by the Rev. Michael Adler, in an essay called "A Medieval Bookworm" (see The Bookworm, ii, 251).

The full title of Mr. Alexander Ireland's book–so much drawn upon in this essay–is "The Book-Lover's Enchiridion, a Treasury of Thoughts on the Solace and Companionship of Books, Gathered from the Writings of the Greatest Thinkers, from Cicero, Petrarch, and Montaigne, to Carlyle, Emerson, and Ruskin" (London and New York, 1894).

Mr. F.M. Nichols' edition of the "Letters of Erasmus" (1901) is the source of the quotation of one of that worthy's letters.

The final quotation comes from the Wisdom of Solomon, ch. vi. v. 12; ch. viii. vv. 2, 16; and ch. ix. v. 4. The "radiance" of Wisdom is, in ch. vii, 26, explained in the famous words, "For she is an effulgence from everlasting light, an unspotted mirror of the working of God, and an image of His goodness."

Medieval Wayfaring

The evidence for many of the statements in this paper will be found in various contexts in "Jewish Life in the Middle Ages," in the Hebrew travel literature, and in such easily accessible works as Graetz's "History of the Jews."

Achimaaz has been much used by me. His "Book of Genealogies" (Sefer Yochasin) was written in 1055. The Hebrew text was included by Dr. A. Neubauer in his "Mediaeval Jewish Chronicles," ii, pp. 114 et seq. I might have cited Achimaaz's account of an amusing incident in the synagogue at Venosa. There had been an uproar in the Jewish quarter, and a wag added some lines on the subject to the manuscript of the Midrash which the travelling preacher was to read on the following Sabbath. The effect of the reading may be imagined.

Another source for many of my statements is a work by Julius Aronius, Regesten zur Geschichte der Juden in Deutschland, Berlin, 1893. It presents many new facts on the medieval Jewries of Germany.

The quaint story of the Jewish sailors told by Synesius is taken from T.R. Glover's "Life and Letters in the Fourth Century" (Cambridge, 1901), p. 330.

A careful statement on communal organization with regard to the status of travellers and settlers was contributed by Weinberg to vol. xii of the Breslau Monatsschrift. The title of the series of papers is Die Organisation der jüdischen Gemeinden.

For evidence of the existence of Communal Codes, or Note-Books, see Dr. A. Berliner's Beiträge zur Geschichte der Raschi-Commentare, Berlin, 1903, p. 3.

Benjamin of Tudela's "Itinerary" has been often edited, most recently by the late M.N. Adler (London, 1907). Benjamin's travels occupied the years 1166 to 1171, and his narrative is at once informing and entertaining. The motives for his extensive journeys through Europe, Asia, and Africa are thus summed up by Mr. Adler (pp. xii, xiii): "At the time of the Crusades, the most prosperous communities in Germany and the Jewish congregations that lay along the route to Palestine had been exterminated or dispersed, and even in Spain, where the Jews had enjoyed complete security for centuries, they were being pitilessly persecuted in the Moorish kingdom of Cordova. It is not unlikely, therefore, that Benjamin may have undertaken his journey with the object of finding out where his expatriated brethren might find an asylum. It will be noted that Benjamin seems to use every effort to trace and afford particulars of independent communities of Jews, who had chiefs of their own, and owed no allegiance to the foreigner. He may have had trade and mercantile operations in view. He certainly dwells on matters of commercial interest with considerable detail. Probably he was actuated by both motives, coupled with the pious wish of making a pilgrimage to the land of his fathers."

For Jewish pilgrims to Palestine see Steinschneider's contribution to Röhricht and Meisner's Deutsche Pilgerreisen, pp. 548-648. My statement as to the existence of a Jewish colony at Ramleh in the eleventh century is based on Genizah documents at Cambridge, T.S. 13 J. 1.

For my account of the Trade Routes of the Jews in the medieval period, I am indebted to Beazley's "Dawn of Modern Geography," p. 430.

The Letter of Nachmanides is quoted from Dr. Schechter's "Studies in Judaism," First Series, pp. 131 et seq. The text of Obadiah of Bertinoro's letter was printed by Dr. Neubauer in the Jahrbuch für die Geschichte der Juden, 1863.

The Fox's Heart

The main story discussed in this essay is translated from the so-called "Alphabet of Ben Sira," the edition used being Steinschneider's (Alphabetum Siracidis, Berlin, 1858).

The original work consists of two Alphabets of Proverbs,– twenty-two in Aramaic and twenty-two in Hebrew–and is embellished with comments and fables. A full account of the book is given in a very able article by Professor L. Ginzberg, "Jewish Encyclopedia," ii, p. 678. The author is not the Ben Sira who wrote the Wisdom book in the Apocrypha, but the ascription of it to him led to the incorporation of some legends concerning him. Dr. Ginzberg also holds this particular Fox Fable to be a composite, and to be derived more or less from Indian originals.

"Marriages Are Made in Heaven"

The chief authorities to which the reader is referred are: Midrash Rabba, Genesis Section 68; Leviticus Section 29; and Numbers Sections 3 and 22. Further, Midrash Tanchuma, to the sections Ki tissa, Mattoth, and Vayishlach; Midrash Samuel, ch. v; Babylonian Talmud, Moed Katon, 18b, and Sotah, 2a.

In Dr. W. Bacher's Agada der Tannaiten, ii, pp. 168-170, will be found important notes on some of these passages.

I have freely translated the story of Solomon's daughter from Buber's Tanchuma, Introduction, p. 136. It is clearly pieced together from several stories, too familiar to call for the citation of parallels. With one of the incidents may be compared the device of Sindbad in his second voyage. He binds himself to one of the feet of a rukh, i.e. condor, or bearded vulture. In another adventure he attaches himself to the carcass of a slaughtered animal, and is borne aloft by a vulture. A similar incident may be noted in Pseudo-Ben Sira (Steinschneider, p. 5).

Compare also Gubernatis, Zool. Myth, ii, 94. The fabulous anka was banished as punishment for carrying off a bride.

For the prayers based on belief in the Divine appointment of marriages, see "Jewish Life in the Middle Ages," ch. x.

One of the many sixteenth century Tobit dramas is Tobie, Comedie De Catherin Le Doux: En laquelle on void comme les marriages sont faicts au ciel, & qu'il n'y a rien qui eschappe la providence de Dieu (Cassel, 1604).

Hebrew Love Songs

From personal observation, Dr. G.H. Dalman collected a large number of modern Syrian songs in his Palästinischer Diwan (Leipzig, 1901). The songs were taken down, and the melodies noted, in widely separated districts. Judea, the Hauran, Lebanon, are all represented. Dr. Dalman prints the Arabic text in "Latin" transliteration, and appends German renderings. Wetzstein's earlier record of similar folk-songs appears in Delitzsch's Commentary on Canticles–Hohelied und Koheleth,–1875 and also in the Zeitschrift für Ethnologie, v, p. 287. Previous commentators had sometimes held that the Song of Songs was a mere collection of detached and independent fragments, but on the basis of Wetzstein's discoveries, Professor Budde elaborated his theory, that the Song is a Syrian wedding-minstrel's repertory.

This theory will be found developed in Budde's Commentary on Canticles (1898); it is a volume in Marti's Kurzer Hand-Commentar zum Alten Testament. An elaborate and destructive criticism of the repertory theory may be read in Appendix ii of Mr. Andrew Harper's "Song of Solomon" (1902): the book forms a volume in the series of the Cambridge Bible for Schools. Harper's is a very fine work, and not the least of its merits is its exposition of the difficulties which confront the attempt to deny unity of plot and plan to the Biblical song. Harper also expresses a sound view as to the connection between love-poetry and mysticism. "Sensuality and mysticism are twin moods of the mind." The allegorical significance of the Song of Songs goes back to the Targum, an English version of which has been published by Professor H. Gollancz in his "Translations from Hebrew and Aramaic" (1908).

Professor J.P. Mahaffy's view on the Idylls of Theocritus may be read in his "History of Greek Literature," ii, p. 170, and in several pages of his "Greek Life and Thought" (see Index, s.v.).

The passage in which Graetz affirms the borrowing of the pastoral scheme by the author of Canticles from Theocritus, is translated from p. 69 of Graetz's Schir ha-Schirim, oder das salomonische Hohelied (Vienna, 1871). Though the present writer differs entirely from the opinion of Graetz on this point, he has no hesitation in describing Graetz's Commentary as a masterpiece of brilliant originality.

The rival theory, that Theocritus borrowed from the Biblical Song, is supported by Professor D.S. Margoliouth, in his "Lines of Defence of the Biblical Revelation" (1900), pp. 2-7. He also suggests (p. 7), that Theocritus borrowed lines 86-87 of Idyll xxiv from Isaiah xi. 6.

The evidence from the scenery of the Song, in favor of the natural and indigenous origin of the setting of the poem, is strikingly illustrated in G.A. Smith's "Historical Geography of the Holy Land" (ed. 1901), pp. 310-311. The quotation from Laurence Oliphant is taken from his "Land of Gilead" (London, 1880).

Egyptian parallels to Canticles occur in the hieroglyphic love-poems published by Maspero in Études égyptiennes, i, pp. 217 et seq., and by Spiegelberg in Aegyptiaca (contained in the Ebers Festschrift, pp. 177 et seq.). Maspero, describing, in 1883, the affinities of Canticles to the old Egyptian love songs, uses almost the same language as G.E. Lessing employed in 1777, in summarizing the similarities between Canticles and Theocritus. It will amuse the reader to see the passages side by side.

Maspero

Il n'y a personne qui, en lisant la traduction de ces chants, ne soit frappé de la ressemblance qu'ils présentent avec le Cantique des Cantiques. Ce sont les mêmes façons ..., les mêmes images ..., les mêmes comparaisons.

Lessing

Immo sunt qui maximam similitudinem inter Canticum Canticorum et Theocriti Idyllia esse statuant ... quod iisdem fere videtur esse verbis, loquendi formulis, similibus, transitu, figuris.

If these resemblances were so very striking, then, as argued in the text of this essay, the Idylls of Theocritus ought to resemble the Egyptian poems. This, however, they utterly fail to do.

For my acquaintance with the modern Greek songs I am indebted to Mr. G.F. Abbott's "Songs of Modern Greece" (Cambridge, 1900). The Levantine character of the melodies to Hebrew Piyyutim based on the Song of Songs is pointed out by Mr. F.L. Cohen, in the "Jewish Encyclopedia," i, p. 294, and iii, p. 47.

The poem of Taubah, and the comments on it, are taken from C.J.L. Lyall's "Translations of Ancient Arabic Poetry, chiefly prae-Islamic" (1885), P. 76.

The Hebrew text of Moses ibn Ezra's poem–cited with reference to the figure of love surviving the grave–may be found in Kaempf's Zehn Makamen (1858), p. 215. A German translation is given, I believe, in the same author's Nichtandalusische Poesie andalusischer Dichter.

Many Hebrew love-poems, in German renderings, are quoted in Dr. A. Sulzbach's essay, Die poetische Litteratur (second section, Die weltliche Poesie), contributed to the third volume of Winter and Wunsche's Jüdische Litteratur (1876). His comments, cited in my essay, occur in that work, p. 160. Amy Levy's renderings of some of Jehudah Halevi's love songs are quoted by Lady Magnus in the first of her "Jewish Portraits." Dr. J. Egers discusses Samuel ha-Nagid's "Stammering Maid" in the Graetz Jubelschrift (1877), pp. 116-126.

George Eliot and Solomon Maimon

The Autobiography of Solomon Maimon (1754-1800) was published in Berlin (1792-3) in two parts, under the title Salomon Maimon's Lebensgeschichte. Moses Mendelssohn befriended Maimon, in so far as it was possible to befriend so wayward a personality. Maimon made real contributions to philosophy.

The description of Daniel Deronda's purchase of the volume is contained in ch. xxxiii of the novel. In Holborn, Deronda came across a "second-hand book-shop, where, on a narrow table outside, the literature of the ages was represented in judicious mixture, from the immortal verse of Homer to the mortal prose of the railway novel. That the mixture was judicious was apparent from Deronda's finding in it something that he wanted–namely, that wonderful piece of autobiography, the life of the Polish Jew, Salomon Maimon."

The man in temporary charge of the shop was Mordecai. This is his first meeting with Deronda, who, after an intensely dramatic interval, "paid his half-crown and carried off his 'Salomon Maimon's Lebensgeschichte' with a mere 'Good Morning.'"

How Milton Pronounced Hebrew

Milton's transliterations are printed in several editions of his poems; the version used in this book is that given in D. Masson's "Poetical Works of Milton," in, pp. 5-11. The notes of the late A.B. Davidson on Milton's Hebrew knowledge are cited in the same volume by Masson (p. 483). Landor had no high opinion of Milton as a translator. "Milton," he said, "was never so much a regicide as when he lifted up his hand and smote King David." But there can be no doubt of Milton's familiarity with the original, whatever be the merit of the translations. To me, Milton's rendering of Psalm lxxxiv seems very fine.

The controversy between the advocates of the versions of Rous and Barton–which led to Milton's effort–is described in Masson, ii, p. 312.

Reuchlin's influence on the pronunciation of Hebrew in England is discussed by Dr. S.A. Hirsch, in his "Book of Essays" (London, 1905), p. 60. Roger Bacon, at a far earlier date, must have pronounced Hebrew in much the same way, but he was not guilty of the monstrosity of turning the Ayin into a nasal. Bacon (as may be seen from the facsimile printed by Dr. Hirsch) left the letter Ayin unpronounced, which is by far the best course for Westerns to adopt.

The Cambridge Platonists

Henry More (1614-1687) was the most important of the "Cambridge Platonists." Several of his works deal with the Jewish Cabbala. More recognized a "Threefold Cabbala, Literal, Philosophical, and Mystical, or Divinely Moral." He dedicated his Conjectura Cabbalistica to Cudworth, Master of Christ's College,

Cambridge, of which More was a Fellow. Cudworth was one of those who attended the Whitehall Conference, summoned by Cromwell in 1655 to discuss the readmission of the Jews to England.

Platonic influence was always prevalent in mystical thought. The Cabbala has intimate relations with neo-Platonism.

The Anglo-Jewish Yiddish Literary Society

The question raised as to the preservation of Yiddish is not unimportant at this juncture. It is clear that the old struggle between Hebrew and Yiddish for predominance as the Jewish language must become more and more severe as Hebrew advances towards general acceptance as a living language.

Probably the struggle will end in compromise. Hebrew might become one of the two languages spoken by Jews, irrespective of what the other language might happen to be.

The Mystics and Saints of India

The full title of Professor Oman's work is "The Mystics, Ascetics, and Saints of India. A Study of Sadhuism, with an account of the Yogis, Sanyasis, Bairagis, and other strange Hindu Sectaries" (London, 1903).

The subject of asceticism in Judaism has of late years been more sympathetically treated than used to be the case. The Jewish theologians of a former generation were concerned to attack the excesses to which an ascetic course of life may lead. This attack remains as firmly justified as ever. But to deny a place to asceticism in the Jewish scheme, is at once to pronounce the latter defective and do violence to fact.

Speaking of the association of fasting with repentance, Dr. Schechter says: "It is in conformity with this sentiment, for which there is abundant authority both in the Scriptures and in the Talmud, that ascetic practices tending both as a sacrifice and as a castigation of the flesh, making relapse impossible, become a regular feature of the penitential course in the medieval Rabbinic literature" ("Some Aspects of Rabbinic Theology," 1909, PP. 339-340).

Moreover, the fuller appreciation of the idea of saintliness, and the higher esteem of the mystical elements in Judaism–ideas scarcely to be divorced from asceticism–have helped to confirm the newer attitude. Here, too, Dr. Schechter has done a real service to theology. The Second Series of his "Studies in Judaism" contains much on this subject. What he has written should enable future exponents of Judaism to form a more balanced judgment on the whole matter.

Fortunately, the newer view is not confined to any one school of Jewish thought. The reader will find, in two addresses contained in Mr. C.G. Montefiore's "Truth in Religion" (1906), an able attempt to weigh the value and the danger of an ascetic view of life. It was, indeed, time that the Jewish attitude towards so powerful a force should be reconsidered.

Lost Purim Joys

The burning of Haman in effigy is recorded in the Responsa of a Gaon published by Professor L. Ginzberg in his "Geniza Studies" ("Geonica," ii, pp. 1-3). He holds that the statement as to the employment of "Purim bonfires among the Babylonian and Elamitic Jews as given in the Aruch (s. v. [Hebrew: shin-vav-vav-resh]) undoubtedly goes back to this Responsum."

On Purim parodies much useful information will be found in Dr. Israel Davidson's "Parody in Jewish Literature" (New York, 1907). See Index s.v. Purim (p. 289).

For a statement of the supposed connection between Purim and other spring festivals, see Paul Haupt's "Purim" (Baltimore, 1906), and the article in the "Encyclopaedia Biblica," cols. 3976-3983. Such theories do not account adequately for the Book of Esther.

Schodt (Jüdische Merkwürdigkeiten, 1713, ii, p. 314) gives a sprightly account of what seems to have been the first public performance of a Purim play in Germany.

Jews and Letters

Leopold Löw investigated the history of writing, and of the materials used among the Jews, in his Graphische Requisiten und Erzeugnisse bei den Juden (2 vols., Leipzig, 1870-71).

On Jewish letter-carriers in Germany, see the article of Dr. I. Kracauer in the "Jewish Encyclopedia," viii, p. 15. The first Post-Jude is named in 1722. These Jewish letter-carriers received no salary from the Government, but collected a fee from the recipients of the letters.

The Talmudic Bê-Davvar [Hebrew: beth-yod-(maqqef)-daleth-vav-aleph-resh] was really a Court of Justice (perhaps a Circuit Court). As, however, davvar meant a despatch-bearer, the phrase Bê-Davvar passed over later into the meaning Post-Office. Davvar seems connected with the root dur, "to form a circle"; the pael form (davvar) would mean "to go around," perhaps to travel with merchandise and letters.

The Shape of Matzoth

In the twentieth chapter of Proverbs v. 17, we find the maxim:

"Bread gained by fraud is sweet to a man,
But afterwards his mouth will be filled with gravel."

The exact point of this comparison was brought home to me when I spent a night at Modin, the ancient home of the Maccabees. Over night I enjoyed the hospitality of a Bedouin. In the morning I was given some native bread for breakfast. I was very hungry, and I took a large and hasty bite at the bread, when lo! my mouth was full of gravel. They make the bread as follows: One person rolls the dough into a thin round cake (resembling a Matzah), while another person places hot cinders on the ground. The cake is put on the cinders and gravel, and an earthenware pot is spread over all, to retain the heat. Hence the bread comes out with fragments of gravel and cinder in it. Woe betide the hasty eater! Compare Lamentations iii. 16, "He hath broken my teeth with gravel stones." This, then, may be the meaning of the proverb cited at the head of this note. Bread hastily snatched, advantages thoughtlessly or fraudulently grasped, may appear sweet in anticipation, but eventually they fill a man's mouth with gravel.

The quotation from Paulus Aringhus' Roma subterranea novissima will be found in vol. ii, p. 533 of the first edition (Rome, 1651). This work, dealing mainly with the Christian sepulchres in Rome, was reprinted in Amsterdam (1659) and Arnheim (1671), and a German translation appeared in Arnheim in 1668. The first volume (pp. 390 et seq.) fully describes the Jewish tombs in Rome, and cites the Judeo-Greek inscriptions. There is much else to interest the Jewish student in these two stately and finely illustrated folios.

www.ingramcontent.com/pod-product-compliance
Lightning Source LLC
Chambersburg PA
CBHW072134160426
43197CB00012B/2107